Advance Praise for
The Uncommon Book of Prayer

"A timely guide to living in a heart-centered, grounded, and fearless way. Vivid and eloquent, with a wide spectrum of different cultural interpretations, methods, and templates to incorporate prayer—a most important, yet underestimated, component of healing."

—LATA CHETTRI-KENNEDY, community herbalist, teacher, and founder of Flower Power Herbs & Roots

"I have never had a relationship to prayer before, and never thought I would. But Heidi's book helped me understand that praying didn't have to be some rote thing I did before sleeping or eating, but rather a continuous conversation with myself and the universe. There is something about both the power and simplicity that this book offers that connected with me so deeply, that the first time I admitted I was praying, I found myself crying the whole time."

—MARISA MELTZER, author of *This Is Big*, *Girl Power*, and *Glossy*

"For years now, Heidi Smith's mission has been to resacralize experience and to rediscover and resurrect hard ancient methods and mysteries and plant them in busy, complex, messy modern life. This astute, encyclopedic, frequently wise book continues that project. It's a gift and a reminder. Much of the time it can seem like prayer is all we have. Maybe—now and again—it's all we need."

—WILLIAM TODD SCHULTZ, PhD, author of *The Mind of the Artist*

This is the book on prayer that I have been waiting for! Inspiring, thoughtfully researched, and beautiful, *The Uncommon Book of Prayer* offers an inclusive and modern approach to the sacred, universal act of prayer."

—NICOLE PIVIROTTO, designer and author of *Prism Oracle* and *Color, Form, and Magic*

"*The Uncommon Book of Prayer* lovingly guides you away from the patriarchal, white supremacist, and heteronormative ideas about prayer, and brings you into a world where prayer is a valuable tool in your arsenal of self-care practices, encouraging you to connect to the divine during moments of joy—not just in moments of desperation—which in turn helps you deepen your relationship with yourself. This book is a beautiful offering to the collective."

**—CLAIRE GOODCHILD, author and artist of *The Book of Ancestors*
and *The Antique Anatomy Tarot***

"Building upon the extraordinary insights of Heidi's first book, *The Uncommon Book of Prayer* is itself a prayer for collective healing co-created through Heidi's devoted attunement to the unseen, divine, ancestral wisdom, and ecological intelligence; and in respectful dialogue with a multiplicity of diverse social and cultural perspectives, traditions, and cosmologies. With so much to feel helpless about at this moment, this book is a timely offering, reminding us of great power in each of us to harness prayer as a means of intentionally committing to interconnectedness, mutuality, solidarity, and love."

—NICOLE DAUNIC, PhD, founder of Black Hole Hollow

"*The Uncommon Book of Prayer* is the awakening we need right now for the healing of self, our communities, and the Earth. This book is a remembrance of our connection to our hearts and souls, Spirit, and each other."

**—LINDA LOPES, Ra Illuminare Multidimensional Healer and
Sacred Drum Practitioner**

"I have always loved the quote, 'Prayer is speaking to God. Meditation is listening to God.' But *The Uncommon Book of Prayer* reminded me that being in a life of prayer is communing with God in every second. That being in *wocekiye* (relationship) is living in love with my heart's communication with and from the Divine."

—GRACE HARRY, author of *The Joy Strategist*

"A beautifully written book that empowers us all to believe prayer can be used to effect change in our lives. I read it late into the night and found myself thinking about it first thing every morning."

—LYDIA FENET, author of *The Most Powerful Woman in the Room Is You*

The
Uncommon
Book
of Prayer

*A Guide to Co-Creating
with the Universe*

HEIDI SMITH

Illustrated by Chelsea Granger

RUNNING PRESS
PHILADELPHIA

Running Press
Hachette Book Group
1290 Avenue of the Americas, New York, NY 10104
www.runningpress.com
@Running_Press

First Edition: October 2024

Published by Running Press, an imprint of Hachette Book Group, Inc.
The Running Press name and logo are trademarks of Hachette Book Group, Inc.

The Hachette Speakers Bureau provides a wide range of authors for speaking events. To find out more, go to www.hachettespeakersbureau.com or email HachetteSpeakers@hbgusa.com.

Running Press books may be purchased in bulk for business, educational, or promotional use. For more information, please contact your local bookseller or the Hachette Book Group Special Markets Department at Special.Markets@hbgusa.com.

The publisher is not responsible for websites (or their content) that are not owned by the publisher. The publisher is not responsible for and does not endorse any organization or website mentioned in this book.

All illustrations courtesy of Chelsea Granger. All photographs courtesy of Heidi Smith unless otherwise noted on p. 258.

Print book cover and interior design by Susan Van Horn

Library of Congress Cataloging-in-Publication Data has been applied for.

ISBNs: 978-0-7624-8577-2 (hardcover), 978-0-7624-8578-9 (ebook)

Printed in Thailand

APS

10   9   8   7   6   5   4   3   2   1

For my Grandmother, Jane

**In solidarity with my prayers for the
Earth, I will be donating 10% of my
royalties earned from the sales of
this book to the National Resources
Defense Council.**

CONTENTS

Introduction

BEFORE PUBLICATION OF MY FIRST BOOK, *THE BLOOM Book: A Flower Essence Guide to Cosmic Balance*, my life was impacted by a confluence of elements. I was debuting as an author during a global pandemic. The United States was plunged into an essential but chaotic racial justice reckoning. I was going through an extremely painful time personally. And I was doing my best to meet the needs of my clients and community during a traumatizing time. Like so many others, I was in the midst of a stressful moment with a lot of unknowns. I was feeling rocked—and also ready for whatever was next.

There were a few things that sustained and even saved me that summer: the foundational healing work I had already realized; my partner and my cats; flowers and nervine herbs; my friends and teachers; the work I was undertaking with my therapist, Sheri Heller; and nature, in all her multidimensional glory. Alongside these familiar and sustaining allies, a new element bloomed within my spiritual practice during this time, which proved to be the most lifesaving of all: prayer.

I've always had a relationship with prayer. However, it took some time for that relationship to blossom into a liberatory practice. When I embarked on my new relationship with prayer, I searched for books to support my exploration. While I did manage to find a few good ones, I longed for something more. I wanted to find texts that felt true and were written from an elevated, interconnected consciousness, beyond the dominant, limited paradigm. I wanted something that spoke to ancient truths and wisdom. Eventually, I arrived at a place many authors reach—I would need to write the book on prayer I was seeking, because it didn't exist yet.

To begin, I want to share my definition of *prayer*.

I define prayer as an active agreement that you make between your soul and the divine (whatever that means to you). It is a sacred practice that can be called upon to bring about states of grace, healing, and change.

For many, *prayer* is a polarizing term. I use prayer interchangeably with *spell*, *mantra*, *affirmation*, and *resonant language*. If any of those words or phrases feel like a better fit for you, use them! *God* is a polarizing term as well, and perhaps you'd rather use *spirit*, *soul*, *universe*, or *divine*.* Perhaps your personal cosmology and beliefs about divinity are evolving and you're not sure which words to use to describe your practice. That's okay, too! Though it need not be, prayer is often associated with religion, which brings up complicated feelings for many. Religious systems have helped, and also harmed, a lot of people. Even so, I encourage you to consider that prayer has been a part of every civilization (pre-colonization), and our misconceptions about it are grounded in the ways it has been stolen, misapplied, and, in many cases, used to thwart the very power it holds to help us. This is not what lies at the true heart of prayer, though.

Prayer is *not* fundamentally a means of control, but it does invite a different relationship between intention and letting go. Prayer *is also*

---

* For simplicity, I have chosen to lowercase these terms, along with: *nature, self, spirit*, and *source*. You may choose to capitalize your own preferred terminology.

not a one-way solicitation for permission or pardon. It is co-creative and relational. As Kierkegaard said, "The function of prayer is not to influence God, but rather to change the nature of the one who prays."

Like many in the West, I was taught that god is a white male entity who lives beyond Earth. In the framework I was given, you can talk to god through prayer whenever you want, but you also need to be afraid of god because "he" controls everything and can be merciless. This framework also stated that god is a being outside of yourself, and to be good enough for this being, you need permission from other mostly white men. I was told that you must continually avow your guilt and culpability, as well as defend your virtue, to be worthy in the eyes of god, because we were all born in sin—especially women, who are responsible for the downfall of humankind. If you were good enough, I learned, you would get to have your prayers answered. If you were not good enough, you would get punished.

I've always felt that prayer did have power attached to it, but I also viewed it as something submissive women quietly did before meals, or whenever they were afraid. I had learned that you prayed mostly out of desperation or despair. I certainly didn't think prayer was cool.

The belief that my divinity resided outside of myself skewed my understanding of my own power. It created an unequal and unnecessary power dynamic between me and my concept of god. At the same time, I can remember lying in bed as a five-year-old and just kind of riffing with god, talking with them like they were a familiar, if somewhat elusive, acquaintance. My relationship with god and prayer further evolved in my twenties. I experienced a dramatic awakening when I lost my brother, Stuart, to suicide, and subsequently embarked on a spiritual tutelage with my teacher Jane Bell. Through our work studying the ancient Egyptian mysteries and the archetypal feminine,* I was reacquainted with a sacred practice that transcended the limited, patriarchal view of god and prayer I had previously known. When I immersed myself in the study of herbal medicine and flower essences, the plant kingdom reintroduced me to prayer on an even deeper, more reverential level. The closer I got to my own heart, the closer I came to god, until I felt no real separation from my divinity at all.

Before *The Bloom Book*'s publication, prayer surrounded me with angelic protection, grace, and a stability that would guide me through an acute healing period and into a new era of my life. The details of my emotional response to this hellish yet transcendent time are less important than the universality of this human experience: the dark night of the soul. There will be times in life where we are pushed to what feels like the threshold of our existence. Some of us have very heavy karmas to clear in this lifetime, especially those of us on spiritual paths. These difficult soul contracts can require us to resolve issues that involve extreme emotional states (grief, loss, shock, terror, depression), testing our will to survive. These intense trials often have the potential to bring about our greatest transformation. And prayer can be a constant support in this soul work that requires so much from us.

As my prayer work deepened, it began to inform my private practice in some dramatic ways. Most of the clients I see as a mental health practitioner—as well as an herbalist and flower essence practitioner—are survivors of complex trauma. Also referred to as Complex-PTSD/C-PTSD, complex trauma is an attachment injury that results from being exposed to harm over an extended period of time, usually in childhood,

---

* Gender in this context is energetic, relating to masculine and feminine energies in nature—it is not a reflection of reinforcing a heteronormative binary. Nature is not exclusively heterosexual; it is queer, and exhibits homosexuality, bisexuality, and intersex traits. The masculine and feminine principles are part of nature, and give rise to the opposition necessary for reproduction and creation.

and severs the heart/source connection. Complex Trauma (CT) also expands the definition of trauma to be more inclusive of emotional or psychological abuse, the impact of which on development, relationships, and overall well-being is increasingly well-documented. CT can be individual, generational, collective, and systemic.

While I don't intend to overly reinforce or over-pathologize trauma, this kind of harm is rampant, and it has devastating impacts on individuals and communities. Up until our present moment, much of it has gone unseen and unresolved. Even so, I believe the collective is adjusting its course to accept our experiences more fully, as we step out of harmful systems and cycles, and heal together. As this happens, we gain the opportunity to be better resourced for the challenges of this time and place, living with hope, joy, and resilience. **Living on this Earth means we will experience heartbreak, but these healing crises also create opportunities for break***throughs.*

Prayer has always been an established part of my private practice. I open every session with a prayer and grounding, and prayer is sacred in my medicine-making rituals. The clients I serve tend toward open-mindedness about prayer. When I first began to suggest collaborating on resonant language to address problematic symptoms and life inquiries, a few of my clients did hold some understandable and warranted skepticism about utilizing prayer as a vehicle for healing. However, most people were receptive to the idea. I found that for those who expressed hesitation, talking through their negative associations and ambivalence around prayer was an important part of taking the power back in this approach.

I started to receive very clear guidance about the relationship between words, specificity of feeling, visualization, and embodiment—and how these elements aid in healing outcomes. A map presented itself

that showed me how to navigate a polarity of self-limiting beliefs and negative speech on one side, and affirmative speech and self-love on the other. Pretty soon, people weren't just talking about change in abstract terms, but were instead rewriting their own internal dialogues with the help of prayer, moving out of the domain of victimization and into a consciousness of co-creation. In my prayer circles and classes, we gained further clarity about the space for possibility and the opportunities for greater resonance that open when we create, think, and speak language that is in coherence, or language that is true, real, and heart-centered.

I have come to believe that some of the methods that have helped client after client in my practice contain the wisdom and power to help all of us in our healing journeys. The process of healing CT involves assisting survivors in reorienting their bodies, minds, and spirits around their inherent wellness and wholeness, rather than their trauma. In essence: We restore the heart/source connection. Both personally and professionally, prayer has revealed itself to me as a potent ally in complex trauma recovery, just as plants had before it. Specifically, it has shown itself to be a helper as we seek to live beyond the lies of the colonized mind we've made manifest—ingrained fallacies such as "I'm not good enough," "There's something wrong with me," and the ever popular "It's not safe to feel good."

Sometimes it's not possible to override our biology with language. But invoking the practice of prayer in concert with the body and the natural world is an alchemical opportunity for fantastic change. With consistency and commitment, the change is more likely. We are all holders of trauma to some extent, and we all have the opportunity to free ourselves by exposing the lies we've been living under. I'm thrilled to share with you new ways to break these spells we've learned to accept as reality, and to share more information on the trauma-prayer connection, in coming chapters.

Prayer has become a constant cosmic companion in my life. I begin my day with prayer. Before meetings, before and after difficult conversations, on holy days, with plants, with animals, and at sacred sites, I pray. Sometimes my friend and colleague, Deborah Bagg, and I lead a class called Dance Prayers, in which we combine intentional movement with prayer. I have been invited to teach on prayer and offer circles at several healing collectives in New York City. I pray with friends, and friends know they can ask me to pray for them, too. Sometimes, there are standby prayers I reach for. Other times, the words just arise spontaneously and flow through me.

There is no shortage of things to feel disheartened about in this world. While worrying is like praying for what you fear, an intentional prayer is a way to bring more agency to those places in your life where you struggle to respond with your higher self. Prayer can serve as an act of solidarity with ourselves, our community, and our Earth. We can choose to exist beyond the limited fear mind. We can choose to live with grace and infinite potential.

When we access that which is asking us for expression in the heart and the soul, and combine this with aligned words and visualizations, we are engaging in a dynamic process of healing. The help arrives, the guidance comes, and the clarity is revealed. We move out of a one-way entreaty and into flow with divine guidance. Plant medicine also works in this relational, co-creative way. Flower essences are an excellent complement to prayer work, as they facilitate change on vibrational levels. In fact, flower essences offer us an expanded understanding of how healing and change happens via wave-function collapse and the extracellular matrix—two concepts that we will explore in the next chapter, What Is Prayer? (see page 17).

This book is a resource to:

Refine your prayer practice.

Explore ambivalence around prayer and some of its difficult associations.

Integrate a prayer practice into co-creative and healing work.

Facilitate prayer circles in your community.

Open and strengthen communication with the heart, our most potent tool of resonance and the seat of true wisdom in the body.

Create space and possibility for hope and dreaming (which are not frivolous, but instead life-sustaining and life-changing practices).

Create vital and creative solutions for your life and our world.

I don't believe that any one way is *the* way. Rather, there are many ways *in* to healing. A conscious prayer practice is a way in to co-creating with the universe and accessing all the gifts that lie therein.

In recent years, science has offered compelling information on the positive impacts of mindfulness on the brain and body, from studies involving mantra, affirmation, meditation, and prayer. While traditional Western science reinforces a linear, mechanistic, and physical reality, newer scientific models reveal expanded perspectives on how energy creates form, how information travels, and how change occurs. Through this book, we will look at some of the emerging neuroscientific theories around prayer that, in many cases, validate the ancient understanding of mindfulness practices and the quantum, interconnected nature of reality.

The guidance of this book builds upon the wisdom of my first book, *The Bloom Book*, which was a call to bring people to the flowers and served as a guide for greater alignment and heart consciousness. This book was my next assignment from the universe: to show people how to pray for themselves in a way that can bring about change and healing in the world. Together, I see both books as a continuing call to and for liberation.

HOW TO USE THIS BOOK

We pray for many reasons. Prayer itself is an act of grace. Even when it's not employed for manifestation, *there is always a purpose to prayer*. The applications for prayer work in healing are as varied and powerful as the imagination will allow. Because whatever you imagine can be made real.

A cosmic law exists, stating that energy follows intention. The prayer guidance I want to share with you in this text is very simple. Here is the formula:

Intention + **language that matches your feeling states** + **visualization and somatic expression** = **positive change**

Language is the agreement we make with our life situations. If you can remain committed to the process of challenging your limiting beliefs (inner duality) and allowing the language of your prayer to evolve—and for you to evolve along with it—potentials are even further realized.

Now, the formula is simple enough, but actually acting on it does require some practice. This text will support you in those practices. It will pull deep insight from the invisible realms in clear, grounded, tangible ways so you can apply those insights to your own prayer work. Each chapter will feature questions, prompts, and creative exercises to engage your right brain (the feminine, intuitive, subconscious side). These are meant to inspire you and encourage deeper study. By the end of this book, you should be well on your way to accessing and sharing heart-centered language that you can use as you are guided to do so.

Remember, every time you pray you are opening up a sacred space. If it feels fitting, you could bring that same sacred energy to the time you spend with this book. Consider saying a prayer or mantra before you begin reading, such as "I will use this book to connect with my inner wisdom." Or "Through this book I will become more aware of how to support myself and my community."

Prayer work can also be enhanced when we allow for divine timing, which runs counter to the linear assumptions of time and space. When we work in the flow of divine timing, we welcome a more cyclical and expansive invitation of change. Try honoring the moon, the solstices and equinoxes, anniversaries, and any days that are holy to you. This text will offer alternative perspectives on space, time, prayer, and healing—because what we believe about all of these things plays a big role in how we feel and how we heal. There is much truth to be found outside the overriding worldview of reality. This book will begin by looking at some of the multicultural purposes of and traditions surrounding prayer, both globally and throughout the ancient world.

Every ancient civilization worshiped the Earth. The trouble began when humans stopped doing what was once natural to us. And that shift has caused serious consequences. We have now entered a time of full ecological collapse. How this plays out remains to be seen, and while the situation is dire, I also believe it is possible for us to hold a vision of the New Earth—where cosmic balance is restored—and make this vision real. Therefore, prayer must be considered an active practice and it must engender our actions in bringing the Earth back into balance immediately.

To the changemakers, justice seekers, wisdom keepers, and true stewards of the land, animals, and elements: My prayers stand with you. May our words and hearts unite to continue lifting up the collective prayers for the New Earth.

So, what can prayer do for you and your community? An empowered prayer practice can:

- **Invite greater connection to what we are creating in the world and how that dream is realized.**

- **Serve to bring about closure to a difficult situation in which physical resolution is not possible.**

- **Bring about greater states of coherence and grace.**

- **Strengthen your connection to a loved one, either here or beyond this plane.**

- **Strengthen your connection to your ancestors.**

- **Enhance your commitment to your own healing work.**

- **Work in attunement with plant medicine and Earth-based practices.**

- **Support existing work involving ritual and any complementary healing modality.**

- **Act as an offering to honor a person, place, memory, or group.**

- **Help wherever you, your community, or our Earth need support.**

While this is not always a safe world, it is possible to feel safe inside yourself—to move through the world with a source connection—and this text outlines ways to integrate prayer to facilitate this process.

When we circle and pray together, the potentials become exponential. The last chapter, Working with Prayer, features elements of prayer, templates, and suggestions for crafting your own prayers and gathering your own prayer circle.

This text exists to provide more context for supporting individual and planetary healing through the power of prayer. Its purpose is to awaken your soul's knowledge of truth. I trust it will reach those souls with whom it is supposed to resonate. It will speak to your intuition and assist in guiding you further on your own unique path, from trusting to knowing, and from knowing into being.

GROUNDING EXERCISE AND PRAYER INTERLUDE

The following exercise and prayer can be called upon whenever you want to access greater presence or protection. I utilize grounding whenever I pray, work with clients, make medicine, or am preparing for a challenging situation.

Grounding Exercise

Sit comfortably, quiet your mind, and close your eyes or lower your gaze, whichever feels right to you. If possible, have your feet flat on the floor or lie down. Take some deep, grounding breaths into your belly and into your root chakra, which is located right around your perineum. Allow the lower part of your body (feet, legs, thighs, and hips) to relax with each exhalation. Feel yourself getting heavy and sinking into your seat. Allow a grounding cord (I like to envision a tree trunk) emanating from your lower back, going through your root chakra, and plunging all the way to the Earth's crystalline core. Feel the Earth energy coming up through your lower body, through your root, and through your feet, with every inhalation. Just notice how you feel in your body as you connect with the Earth. Feel her energy holding you and bringing you into presence. Stay and hang out here for a few minutes if it feels comfortable.

When you feel ready to come back, gently release the grounding cord back to the Earth, and allow your root chakra to come to a comfortable, neutral position. Slowly deepen your breath once again, bring your awareness back to your space, and open your eyes.

Complex trauma survivors usually need to relearn how to quiet the mind. The dorsal, or backside, of the vagus nerve responds to danger that may be either real or perceived. When our dorsal vagal goes into protection mode, it shuts down, or freezes. When this happens, we may disassociate, feeling trapped or numb. In some instances, meditation and prayer can exacerbate dorsal vagal shutdown. If this is an issue for you, you can integrate soft music or another gentle sensory stimulus like ambient music, a sensory toy (I have a magic wand filled with glitter), a somatic exercise like tapping the forearms or, if seated, gently rocking side to side on the sitz bones. I do feel it's beneficial to build your tolerance for presence, stillness, and quiet, at whatever capacity and pace that feels doable for you.

GROUNDING PRAYER

Dear mother/father god, spirit, and universe,

I ask permission to call on the powers of my highest self, light, love, truth, nature, and healing.

I call on all my angels, guides, and ancestors.

I call on the energies of Mother Earth and Tree Spirits.

I allow my energy to root down into the center of the Earth.

My mind is at peace, and all thoughts wanting my attention float away like clouds.

I am anchored in perfect presence.

I am rooted in acceptance of all that is.

I allow all of my chakras to align with the heartbeat of the Earth.

I am connected to all life through this divine rhythm.

I feel the warm, nourishing, and healing energy of Mother Earth, holding me in balance.

Thank you so much for all that you do for us, Mother Earth.

With deepest gratitude, so be it.

Flower essences to complement this prayer:
red cedar, red clover, corn

What Is Prayer?

MANY IN THE WEST THINK OF PRAYER AS ASKING FOR HELP. We often assume that someone or something is intervening on our behalf, to make our wishes or fervent hopes come true. But what is prayer really? Why do we do it? To whom are we praying? What needs to be changed to make us feel as though our prayers have been answered—outside circumstances, ourselves, or both? We will explore these questions together. This chapter will outline some ways to rethink prayer as a means for connection, discovery, and change. This book is more concerned with the *how of prayer*, but in order to cover this terrain thoughtfully, we need to first delve into the *what* and *why of prayer*. Here, I will offer a holistic and inclusive way to think about what prayer is and why we do it. My goal is to encourage open-mindedness and inquiry, hopefully leading you to feel inspired to contemplate what prayer can mean and look like in your life.

> **"Prayer is listening to the silence of one's own heart."**
>
> —MOTHER TERESA

DEFINING PRAYER

I've been led to explore prayer through people and practices from a variety of influences, including: Christianity, Tibetan Buddhism, Native American spirituality and shamanism, Celtic Scottish wisdom traditions, European folk and pagan traditions, and ancient Egyptian mysticism. I am a middle-aged, cisgender, heterosexual, Euro-American white woman. My identifiers, personal experience, and biases are all going to impact how I think about and write on this subject.

While my own experience and thoughts are personal, prayer itself is universal. It occurs in all cultures. It belongs to all people, beyond race or religion. That said, the majority of the literature in the West that has been written about prayer has come from an Abrahamic tradition, led by Christianity, then Judaism and Islam. I am more drawn to the mystical branches of the Abrahamic religions, and I want to honor these traditions, while also examining prayer outside of the Abrahamic context—and outside of religion altogether, from a secular perspective.

There are differences and similarities between the way a devout Catholic, a Buddhist, and a pan-spiritual seeker like myself might define prayer. To honor prayer as a healing practice, we must acknowledge its many interpretations, especially from those traditions that have been historically othered, denigrated, or erased by more dominant cultures. I'm interested in *the similarities between* historical prayer practices, because I think these common threads elucidate how our humanity and liberation are cosmically linked. Additionally, I see a lot of value in restoring connection to those customs related to the feminine, which predate much of the monotheistic (and often patriarchal) ideologies that prevail over our consciousness, including how we understand prayer. For, in the words of author and Jungian analyst Jean Shinoda Bolen, "As long as what is considered sacred is always in the image of men, a whole aspect of what divinity is for women is not accessible to us."

There are many ways to interpret prayer through the various sciences: evolutionarily, biologically, anthropologically, theologically, socially, and psychologically. Let us consider that these branches of understanding hold some clues to understanding prayer, but they could never grasp in totality the *what* and *why* of prayer. Whose words do we honor—the Western scientist with numerous credentials? Or the unpublished fifth-generation medicine woman? Who gets to define what is valid?

Beyond both religion and science, there is also the subjective, lived experience necessary to honor our own meaning. I hope the sliver of perspective I offer you in this chapter will encourage you to consider different angles and possibilities, ultimately leading you to trust your own intuition and experience with prayer.

Once again, here is the definition of prayer that I offer: **Prayer is an active agreement that you make between your soul and the divine (whatever that means to you). It is a sacred practice that can be called upon to bring about states of grace, healing, and change.**

I hope this information helps you define prayer for yourself. It is, of course, completely fine to allow your definition to evolve. Perhaps you don't need to define it at all. You can just let it flow.

> *"Attention, taken to its highest degree, is the same thing as prayer.*
> *It presupposes faith and love."*
>
> —SIMONE WEIL

Definitions of Prayer from Around the World

In Sanskrit/Hindi, पूरारूथना, *or **prārthanā**, means to pray and can also mean a number of other things including appeal, invoke, and communion.*

———

*In Aramaic, the word for **pray** is **tselutha**, which can be interpreted to mean being "totally covered," the way a blanket covers a bed.*

———

*In Arabic, the word that means to pray is debated, but one interpretation is the term **Salah**, which means "linking things together."*

———

*Though not a direct translation, the related idea of **Dadirri**, from the Australian Aboriginal peoples, is the "inner deep listening and quiet still awareness with oneself and the land."*

———

*In Hebrew, **lahitpallel** means "to pray, as well as to judge oneself."*

———

*In Greek, **proseuche** is a common term for prayer in the New Testament, and it roughly translates to "a vow, and a close relationship with god."*

———

*In Yoruba, **gbadura** means to pray and also "to address a deity, or to call upon in supplication."*

———

*In Norse, **bön** means to pray and "to communicate with one's god."*

In Mandarin Chinese, 禱告, *or **dǎo gào**, means to pray and also "a spiritual communion with god."*

*In Navajo, **sodilzin** means "to petition to a higher being."*

*In Lakota, **wocekiye** means to pray and "to claim relationship with."*

Prayer can be mystical or seemingly mundane. It can be something done at certain times or on an ongoing basis, as living a prayer. Prayer is something we can call upon at any time, in any place, and for any purpose. It can accompany any marker of life, experience, or emotional state. It may be something we practice spontaneously or consistently—the latter of which we'll explore at length.

"Prayer has a language, a dialogue, and many times an offering, a ritual to make this contact or connection with this source of LOVE. It activates our heartfelt desires for the good of the all, and can summon the 'all that is' to guide us, inspire us, and help us achieve more fully the experience of oneness, expansion, and fulfillments of our personal and global destiny."

—VIRGINIA VORONIN

A Prayer Can Be . . .

Spoken Words: *psalm, poem, spell, incantation, meditation, mantra, affirmation, invocation, illumination, rite*

Silence and Stillness: *mindfulness, meditation, contemplation, reflection*

Musical: *chanting, kirtan, hymn; with instruments: bell, cymbals, gong, drums, singing bowls*

Movement: *dancing, whirling, bowing, kneeling, prostrating, anointing, blessing oneself, trance state*

Art: *painting, drawing, sand mandalas, flower arranging, tea ceremony*

Event: *vigil, service, circle, ritual or rite, devotion, medicine making, initiation, anniversary, feast day, harvest, death, birth*

Part of a Healing Modality: *shamanic journey, vision quest, medicine making, spiritual bathing*

A Prayer Can Happen in . . .

a temple, a church, a temescal, a meetinghouse,
your bathtub, nature

A Prayer Can Happen with . . .

a chief, shaman, guide, pastor, rabbi, sheikh, only oneself,
a friend or group, plants, animals

Prayer Can Be Accompanied by Sacred Objects . . .

candles, incense, feathers, stones, clothing, a prayer mat,
holy books, ribbons, flags, *despachos*

You Can Pray with or to . . .

god, spirit, universe, nature, your heart, the elements, gods,
goddesses, saints, angels, ancestors, energies, animal spirits,
plant spirits, planets, stars, constellations

> *"Prayer is a way of communicating through the feminine back brain, the cerebellum, the unconscious. . . . It is a natural waveform that flows through the heart."*
>
> —SEREN AND AZRA BERTRAND

Personally, I've had the good fortune to experience prayer in many ways and in many places. I recall when I visited the Vatican in college and saw Michelangelo's *Pietà* in person. It remains the most awe-inspiring piece of art I've ever encountered. It's so exquisite it doesn't look real—it looks of heavenly origin. I wonder if creating something as astonishing as that is a high exercise in faith, of honoring the divine, or of channeling divinity itself.

I can also feel myself with my teacher, Jane Bell, in Egypt, standing on the shore of the Nile, reconnecting with both magic and pieces of myself that exist beyond this time and place. I think of myself making medicine, writing words of personal devotion and emancipation with my clients, and holding the light of prayer with friends in need. I remember praying alongside the healing waters with the nuns at the Tidrum nunnery in Tibet, where they have vowed to live their whole lives as a prayer for the liberation of humanity. The energy in that space made me feel as if I were in an altered state, and maybe I was. I meditate on sitting in a circle with a fourth-generation medicine man, Carlos, in Oaxaca, feeling so much love from his prayers and in his presence that I could emotionally fall apart and be held completely.

While these unique experiences with prayer have informed my own journey, the location of prayer doesn't need to be exotic. Some of my most powerful experiences have been lying in bed, sitting on a couch with a friend, or in session with a client in my office.

Prayer is the first place I turn when I need help, because it is always accessible no matter where I am or what I'm doing. Prayer is what I can offer people—confidently—when they need help. Prayer can be a powerful offering to people, the plant and animal kingdoms, the elements, and the Earth itself. It is a call for healing and change—especially when it is coupled with action. I would never think to lead a session or workshop without first offering up a prayer to set the space. Just as I've learned to let go of control and trust in the medicine of the plants I work with, I've come to trust the power of prayer with total faith.

On a more internal level, prayer has shown me what is possible in my own healing and evolution. Prayer is a powerful tool when we are open to challenging our perceptions and subconscious internal dialogue. It proves to me again and again that what I speak to myself and write in my journal has energetic weight and attraction potential. Prayer has taught me to be careful about what I reinforce with my words, both spoken and written. It has revealed a new alchemy of possibility, a map of how we can use our higher sensory awareness not against ourselves, but in alignment with our hearts.

The ways we talk with ourselves can be overly critical, fear-based, and even dysmorphic. Prayer teaches me (and this is very much a work in progress!) that I can communicate with my own being in a way that's thoughtful and loving. I can speak to myself the way my loved ones speak to me. Prayer also reminds me that I am not omnipotent—I don't always have answers, but something bigger than me does. This communication is part of a blueprint of universal balance and it is vital for a secure heart attachment with oneself. When this connection is restored, it sets us up for a very different experience of life in this world than the one we may have been conditioned to expect.

Prayer means all of these things to me. It has been a golden thread woven into the fabric of my spiritual life, and it is one of my deepest allies in my evolution as a human and a helper.

Prayer and the Care Bear Stare

Prayer is a very intimate subject for me and for many of us, so I'd like to share a story of how I've personally come to understand why we pray.

When I was a little girl, I loved the Care Bears. Care Bears, if you're not familiar, are adorable, colorful plush bears, each with their own personality based on a particular virtue. Their names, like Share Bear and Cheer Bear, match those traits. If you read the books or watched the cartoons, you learned that to defeat one of their enemies or to help a friend, the Care Bears could, together, transmit a loving stream of energy through their bellies. This light created a ray of love that transformed the heart of their target, waking them up to the truth and their own goodness.

I remember watching the Care Bear movie when I was five or six years old and feeling transfixed when they channeled their energy to help a young boy named Nicholas, who had been under the spell of an evil spirit. As the bears held hands and streamed love from their bellies, I actually wept. It was the first time I'd ever cried watching a movie. I was probably having an emotional response for several reasons, but I do remember thinking, "Grown-ups probably don't believe in this. They think this is stupid." In that moment, though, I told myself that I would make the Care Bear stare real. I would choose to remember this feeling and make it real, even if other people didn't believe.

> *"Prayer can be like drawing water from a well and also*
> *like a rainfall that you simply receive in your heart."*
>
> —ST. TERESA OF ÁVILA

When I look back on little Heidi watching that movie, I don't see a silly kid experiencing a fantasy. Instead, I feel a young child highly attuned to the spirit world confronting something that felt powerful, true, and real. I think I knew that cartoons were make-believe, but the power to harness the frequency of love to heal seemed totally obvious to me. For me—and I feel really lucky for this to be the case—the reason why I prayed was established before I could be impacted by too much cultural conditioning. To me, the purpose was already quite clear: to send and receive love.

I separated from this knowing for some time, when my own heart connection was severed. But later, as an adult in my late thirties, this gnosis returned as I began fully returning to myself. This reconnection required that I learn a lot about healing, experience different kinds of love and loss, and ultimately let go of a lot of my own judgments, intellectualizations, and assumptions about what *I thought I knew* about love and energy. When I did, I arrived at the realization that the child had known all along.

THE UNIVERSALITY OF PRAYER— AND WHAT WE CAN LEARN FROM IT

People from all different religious and philosophical traditions pray. According to a Pew Research Center survey, nine out of ten Americans pray, and of that number, roughly half pray daily. This is interesting when viewed in contrast with the decline in formal religious affiliation in North America (a trend also reflected globally). Prayer appears to be more popular with older Americans, and it is less popular as a practice in "nones," or those with no religious affiliation.

There are myriad reasons for prayer: birth, death, initiation, transition, blessing, feast, thanksgiving, protection, celebration, a community need or action, a private intercession, communion, confession, praise, listening, guidance, forgiveness, welcoming things in, or letting things go. Prayer can range from grand public displays to private and closed practices, from formal to casual. It may be employed in deep, regular devotion or spontaneously. Prayer held tremendous significance in the ancient world, as evidenced by the rites and ceremonies in prehistoric illustrations on cave walls, stone carvings, and Earth sculptures. Contemporary presentations of prayer link us to our origins, connecting us to fundamental energies of the cosmos and our primordial selves.

In the Catholic tradition the purpose of prayer falls into one of four categories: adoration, contrition, thanksgiving, or supplication. Elsewhere, prayer can serve as an intermediary between humans and those forces that can grant new life, as in Maasai culture. Maasai women prostrate themselves with an *olkereti*, an amulet for good luck, in order to be blessed with a child. In Shintoism, prayers commonly happen at shrines—at home or in public—and may be accompanied by physical offerings, such as coins, to venerate kami, or deities.

In Hinduism, prayer is known as puja, and it is an expression of devotion, or *bhakti*. Prayer in a devotional sense can be practiced as yoga, meditation, and mantras. Also in Hinduism, prayer may be practiced with mudras—specific positioning of the hands and fingers—to enter a particular state of consciousness and also to invoke various deities. In Yoruba tradition, prayers are offered as praise to the Òrìṣà, or deified natural forces, which mediate between humankind and the supernatural. During Ramadan, some Muslims stay up all night praying, completely devoting themselves to worship.

Buddhist chants are analogous to prayers and may be recited as an offering, as a devotional, as a form of instruction, or to prepare for meditation. In the Vajrayana tradition, one might envision a particular mandala and chant *Om mani padme hum*, which is associated with Avalokitesvara, bodhisattva of compassion, and translates to "Praise to the jewel in the lotus."

> *"One should only pray that another would have enough strength to shoulder his burden. If you do that, you lend him some of your own strength."*
>
> —ETTY HILLESUM

Tibetan butter lamp

Cairns were ancient burial mounds and can be found all over the world.
This one is from Slockavullin, Scotland.

Prayer in Antiquity

We can learn about how prayer may have looked and functioned in the ancient world through sacred sites, artwork, and, later, written text. It is easier to observe places of worship in the ancient world than it is to find written prayer, as text appears to have only emerged sometime around the third millennium BCE.

It is impossible to pinpoint when humans began praying, but ancient burial rituals offer hints at the origins of early religious thought. Some of the earliest examples of written prayer are the Assyrian and Babylonian hymns and litanies from Mesopotamia, in what is modern-day Iraq.

As a student of the ancient Egyptian mysteries, I have a particular interest in predynastic Egypt, or the period of time in Egypt prior to 3000 BCE. All facets of life in this ancient civilization were imbued with spiritual significance. Hymns and prayers in ancient Egypt were written on papyri and temple walls, usually to honor particular deities. Individual

Seshat, Dendur, Egypt

prayers may have asked for help, a blessing, guidance, or forgiveness for wrongdoing. *The Egyptian Book of the Dead*, a funerary text containing magic spells to assist the journey through Duat, or the underworld, into the afterlife, could be interpreted as one long prayer.

Women in ancient Egypt were educated, which reflected the masculine-feminine pan-gender diversity within the neteru pantheon (neters were deities, and the word *neter* translates to "nature"). Many know that Thoth was the god of writing, and it was Seshat, also a scribe, who was thought to be the inventor of writing. She was the goddess of writing and wisdom. Seshat is depicted with a seven-pointed flower or star above her head, as well as a writing utensil. As "ruler of books" it would have been her role to transcribe the words of the pharaohs and to protect sacred texts. As I was writing this book, Seshat became a guide for me, and part of my spirit team. If you seek guidance in your writing, and feel a connection to her, you could call her in and ask for help.

In East Asia, ancestor worship can be traced back to the end of the Zhou dynasty (1122–256 BCE), when Taoism emerged in ancient China. Ancestor veneration remains an important practice, connecting the living family with the deceased ancestors. Prayer and rituals honor the deceased and keep them happy in the spiritual world. In return, the ancestors bless and look after the family. Ikebana, the prayerful act of arranging flowers in modern-day Japan, may have ancient spiritual roots, ascribed to early Buddhist saints, who "gathered the flowers strewn by the storm and, in their infinite solicitude for all living things, placed them in vessels of water."

In the British Isles, ancient Celts and Druids performed ceremonies in oak groves and natural shrines, called nemetons, leaving votive offerings in places on the land such as wells or springs, which were believed to serve as portals to the otherworld.

In Australia, Aboriginal prayers and rituals were invoked to allow a person to enter "dreamtime," or the period of time when all life was created. They were performed near sacred sites such as a cave or a spring, to please the spirits and allow one to stay alive.

Ixchel was the jaguar goddess of the Maya, who lived in what is now modern-day Mexico and Central America. Women would pray to her for fertility on the sixth day of the moon.

I connect with my spiritual practice and research in Vermont, which is the homeland of the Abenaki, Wabanaki, and Pennacook Native American Indians. Like many Native American tribes, the Abenaki hold a deep reverence for the Earth and all sentient beings. Their practice includes greeting the sun each day and offering a prayer to the first drink of water. If healing is needed, they may pray to the plants, animals, and rocks for help.

Abenaki couple, eighteenth century

Similar to today, prayers in the ancient world were reflections of the varying religious or philosophical beliefs and devotional practices to which they were tied. Belief systems from this time were likely to be polytheistic and animistic. The ancients worshiped the masculine, feminine, and gods/deities/forces beyond a gender binary. Women and gender queer individuals commonly held spiritually significant positions in many ancient societies. Many indigenous traditions had no specific word for prayer. One interpretation for this could be that prayer was not a discrete concept in many ancient cosmologies. In most cases, prayer was built into aspects of daily life, such as bathing, weaving, hunting, planting, and harvesting. There was little, if any, distinction between magic and prayer, and magical practices were usually accompanied by ritual. The symbol of the circle is a resounding theme across these cultures: of the life cycle, the wheel of the year, the integrated relationship between mind, body, and spirit, of the feminine, and of the group gathering together.

Changing Perspectives on Prayer

Throughout history, civilizations have sought influence and control: of people, resources, and belief systems, as well as how those systems are reinforced through ritual and prayer. Imperialism, colonialism, and colonization transformed the ancient world of prayer. This shift was driven by the rise of the aristocracy and church in Europe. All facets of indigenous and ancient religions—prayer circles, temples, rites, holy days, myths and lore, symbolism—were condemned with increasing zeal throughout the Middle Ages. This included the denunciation of pagan and folk healing traditions, which would be recategorized as witchcraft and evil. Anything regarded as anti-Christian was considered heretical, and the bounds of this perspective spread as European empires exerted their dominion over the Earth.

This was the birth of the dominant paradigm, which redefined prayer. Prayer's new conception was influenced more by linearity and disconnection than it had been previously. We entered the time of the sun—a time characterized by possession and separation. During this arc of time, the feminine, the physical body, and nature become demonized, divinity was separated from life, and the sacred often became something exclusionary—or it was banished altogether.

This slice of time in Europe was a radical reformation of consciousness, which I believe still informs a tension we experience in our beliefs: between ancient and contemporary, between the immaterial and material, between the sacred and scientific. It creates a lot of questions for each of us in our relationship to prayer and how it functions. We will return to this area of inquiry throughout the book.

> **"A balance should be struck between the medieval idea of wholly depending on God and the modern way of sole reliance on the ego."**
>
> —PARAMAHANSA YOGANANDA

Honoring the Mystery

When we study prayer throughout history, we should be mindful that not all sacred practices have been recorded through written language. The West is prone to worship the written word, while discrediting other forms of transmission such as oral tradition, dance, art, and ceremony. There is much wisdom that has been transmitted beyond written documentation, often intentionally so, to keep it hidden and protected. Not all records are meant to be claimed and controlled.

When we reach into the past to explore the origins of prayer, we are getting very close to the essential mystery and the secrets of the universe the ancients may have known. Concepts like time and space become fuzzy. We may try to put words to the ineffable, but by design, the numinous cannot be named. There seem to be more questions than answers. My teacher Jane would remind me, here, that we can become overly attached to the quest for knowledge, grasping for answers to the unanswerable. Especially for Westerners, the desire to define, categorize, and construct is strong. Through prayer, we are invited to let go of the need to know with our intellectual minds, and instead to reconnect with a knowing via our intuition and instinct—domains of our subtle senses and ancestral wisdom.

LAKOTA PRAYER

Wakan-Tanka, Great Mystery,
teach me how to trust
my heart,
my mind,
my intuition,
my inner knowing,
the senses of my body,
the blessings of my spirit.
Teach me to trust these things
so that I may enter my Sacred Space
and love beyond my fear,
and thus Walk in Balance
with the passing of each glorious Sun.

While the history of prayer is clearly linked to religion, its contemporary and healing applications need not be. As a heuristic tool, it is a means for investigation and discovery. Prayer can be a path of deep inquiry, devotion, and service. Given the research that is emerging around the benefits of meditation, mindfulness, and spiritual praxis, when the definition of prayer is expanded to include these disciplines, the data is even more compelling.

> *"When we pray, I think that we can be led to the knowledge of how to meet our next challenge, whatever it is—whether it's physical, psychological, practical, social."*
>
> —MAYA ANGELOU

LANGUAGE, THOUGHT, REALITY— THE NEUROSCIENCE OF PRAYER

I am happy to report that the science on prayer is very good! Of course, specific definitions of what constitutes prayer vary. And though it is not quantifiable the way a medication or measurable treatment is, we can observe the effects of prayer in a neuroscientific context by studying its impacts on our minds under the umbrella of mindfulness, meditation, spiritual and religious practices, and mystical experiences. While phenomenological literature on these subjects has increased in the last two decades, there is still a lack of integrative theoretical models, specifically as they relate to differentiating between spirituality and religiousness. Even so, I've found both the quality and quantity of data on the positive outcomes of meditation and mindfulness, specifically, to be strong.

There are numerous studies that positively correlate meditation and mindfulness with everything from improved control over binge eating to improved sleep to reduction in chronic pain. Neuroimaging (SPECT, PET, and MRI) is an objective measure that provides us with fascinating insight into the physical effects of meditative states on hormonal, immunological, cardiac, respiratory, and nervous system functioning in the body. Activities involving meditation, prayer, and spiritual practice offer both short- and long-term benefits, and have the potential to create permanent changes in both the brain and body.

Scientists have determined that praying involves the medial prefrontal and posterior cingulate cortexes—deep parts of the brain involved in self-reflection and self-soothing. Self-reflection and soothing may not sound like dramatic processes, but these are huge factors in emotional regulation. The ability to create a coherent narrative around your experiences is essential for reprocessing and releasing trauma. Self-soothing is foundational to adaptively working through stress. It is one of the earliest goals of a secure attachment in humans, and those who didn't benefit from the conditions necessary to achieve this milestone in early childhood do have the opportunity to develop this ability later in life. Prayer is one way to go about this repair.

Comparably, spirituality and meditative practices appear to stimulate the production of oxytocin, a hormone and neuropeptide critical for social bonding that is associated with trust, empathy, positive communication, and relaxation. It has also been linked to reducing fear in humans, as well as increasing generosity. Prayer has a positive impact on dopamine, a neurochemical responsible for feeling motivation and pleasure, and serotonin, a neurotransmitter that helps us feel happy and at peace.

We can train our minds, through prayer and meditative practices, as we do our physical bodies. So how much time should we dedicate to our prayer practices if we want to feel the benefits? As with exercise, science points to greater emotional and physical outcomes when prayer and meditation are employed consistently and for longer periods of time. Also like exercise, when you stop, the benefits fade. Andrew Newberg is a leading researcher in the field of the neuroscience of religious and spiritual practices. He's the author of numerous papers and the book *How God Changes Your Brain: Breakthrough Findings from a Leading Neuroscientist*. Newberg (who isn't sure if he believes in a god himself) found that engaging in twelve minutes of personal reflection and prayer each day has a profound impact on the brain, enhancing empathy and compassion and counteracting problematic emotions like anger.

Scientists used to think our brain grew to a certain point and then started to deteriorate. But we now know that the human brain is much more adaptive than that. It can continue to develop and grow with our experiences, and how we choose to repeat or engage with our memories. Evidence suggests that prayer is protective to the aging brain, significantly improving memory, cognition, mood, and overall mental health. And given the way prayer and meditation can strengthen the basal ganglia, movement-based meditations may strengthen brains that are specifically susceptible to age-related diseases like Parkinson's and Alzheimer's.

Spiritual practice isn't just healthy for the brain. It also provides the brain a tremendous opportunity to change and grow. All adaptive changes within the brain can be understood as *neuroplasticity*, or the ability of the brain to restructure itself in response to a wide variety of both positive and negative stimuli. Meditating on or studying any subject is good for the brain, but when we immerse ourselves in spiritual contemplation, we strengthen a "unique neural circuit that specifically enhances social awareness and empathy while subduing destructive feelings and emotions." This is a higher order of thinking and processing, allowing us to adaptively and creatively respond to conflict, which is a tremendous resource in our ever-intensifying world.

We're learning more about the benefits of mystical and transcendent experiences through the clinical use of psychedelics, which are being increasingly applied in primary care settings, and where a single session may be hailed as just as effective—or even more effective—than years of consistent psychotherapy. To a greater extent, when prayer practices are employed in tandem with psychedelics like psilocybin, potentially significant and enduring positive changes in psychological functioning can occur, including "decreased anxiety and fearfulness, and increased feelings of peace/harmony, joy/intense happiness, inter-personal closeness, gratitude, life meaning/purpose, forgiveness, and death acceptance."

Prayer can also create a decrease in activity in the prefrontal cortex, the area of the brain responsible for higher cognitive functions, self-reflection, temporal integration, and memory. While this may not sound positive at the outset, it offers tremendous opportunity for self-expansion. When the prefrontal cortex enters this state, one's sense of self dissolves, which can enhance an intention to reach specific goals. Psychologist Mihaly Csikszentmihalyi referred to this optimal state as *flow*. Csikszentmihalyi found that people are most content, confident, produc-tive, and creative when they are in a state of flow. When we enter flow, our sense of time and space can become distorted (in a good way), our self-consciousness decreases, our brains become more flexible, and we are more open to intra-communication, creating more freely. This is a state associated with self-actualization, and prayer can help you get there.

Deafferentation is a curious form of neural activity precipitated by prayer and meditation, which occurs when "one part of the brain ignores information being sent to it by other parts." This can lead to a radical alteration of perception. Strikingly, it can also enable the prayer or the meditator to voluntarily influence "nonconscious" parts of the brain—or parts of the brain we previously thought were dormant. Deaf-ferentation initiates a neural cascade, activating structures in both hemispheres of the brain, and appears to conclude in the pineal gland, which, in addition to producing melatonin necessary for regulating our circadian rhythms, is the site of the brain's dimethyltryptamine, or DMT, production, which is linked to mystical experiences. This process may explain how, with practice, we gain the ability to reshape our self-concept, worldview, and trans-self-experiences like oneness.

One might assume that the data reinforces prayer and mindfulness as more of a passive practice with moderate benefits, but the science suggests something much stronger. Prayer and spiritual practice create substantial, measurable physical changes, not just in the mind but in the body, too. And the research is only beginning to emerge. In applying intentional prayer as a heuristic practice consistently and over time, we are in effect creating cognitive and somatic frameworks for great healing and change.

Neuropeptides and Addiction

Neuropeptides are chemical formations created in the hypothalamus, the part of the brain responsible for emotional activity. They are responsible for the states of consciousness and feelings we experience. Neuropeptides are created when we have an emotional response to something—good or bad—and the more intense the response, the bigger the dose of chemicals. Every feeling creates a unique neuropeptide signature that then gets flushed into the bloodstream and absorbed by your cells. Every emotion has a vibrational signature, and therefore a particular frequency. Deepak Chopra describes the process of thoughts moving with neuropeptides as "a transformation of non-matter into matter," meaning our emotions create physical effects in our bodies.

When a specific feeling (or set of feelings) are regular or chronic, your cells then become accustomed to needing the same configuration consistently in order to maintain homeostasis, and a dependency is formed. A person will experience craving and withdrawal if the cells are not getting a consistent dose of these chemicals. This sequence is identical whether the neuropeptides are coming from food, sex, drugs, relationships, or from some other internal or external experience. This means that you can become addicted to any feeling state: anxiety, depression, chaos, or calm. In my opinion, this "feeling dependency" significantly impacts your emotional baseline, or what your mood defaults to. This scientific advance greatly benefits the efficacy of treatment models for drug, alcohol, and eating disorder recovery, and we can utilize this finding to help us better understand how repetitive thoughts and language can help us heal, and how we can bring this awareness into our prayer work.

At a cellular level, we become physically dependent on certain feeling states via the neuropeptide loop. This sequence can be something intrinsically generated, and therefore, we can think of this process as co-creative. We can also apply it to our feeling states, and the corresponding beliefs, thoughts, and behaviors related to them. When I am writing and saying my prayers (and this goes for any healing or reparative activity), I think about how my body is creating its own healing imprint every time I engage in this practice.

> **"Indians believe that one cannot fool the spiritual world by uttering words that contradict what is in one's heart, what one intends. Indians often pray silently, with their thoughts, because they believe that, in effect, our thoughts are what we are."**
>
> —JACK D. FORBES, POWHATAN-RENAPÉ AND
> DELAWARE-LENÁPE ELDER

We now know that we carry the epigenetic markers for many generations within us. We also know that while our DNA may define much of how we function, we can influence the expression of a portion of our genetic material, not with artificial intelligence, but with the choices we make in our thoughts, beliefs, and behaviors. We may have inherited coding and neuropeptide patterns that predispose us to more difficult neurochemical experiences in this lifetime, but we also have a choice in how these codes and patterns are expressed.

I have one caveat to offer along with this information. Neuropeptide addiction takes attachment in the Buddhist sense to another level. Attachment to any particular feeling state, whether it be ecstatic bliss or crippling stress (yes, people can definitely become attached and addicted to stress), is problematic. It's problematic because, in nature, change is constant. This extends to our physical and emotional rhythms, as well. Is it nice to feel "better," more joyful, and at peace? Of course. Do we deserve it? Absolutely. But where might you actually be seeking a constant high? Because that isn't sustainable, or natural, and to be overly identified with any state is a setup for more pain, leaving you striving for an illusion. I'm not saying you shouldn't pray for peace—I pray for this daily. But I'm also aware of my grip on it. In the words of Zen Buddhist philosopher and poet Dōgen Zenji, "If you want to travel the way of buddhas and Zen masters, then expect nothing, seek nothing, and grasp nothing."

We know that acts of prayer and meditation bring about physical changes in the brain that promote greater feelings of well-being, relaxation, and contentment. So, it makes sense that we would become habituated to this practice, and we can use this natural neurochemical process to our advantage. In this sense, to think it is to feel it, eventually know it in our bodies, and become it.

"WORRYING IS PRAYING FOR WHAT YOU DON'T WANT." —Bhagavan Das

Worrying uses up a lot of energy that could go toward more gratifying things. There are times when worry is excessive and other times when it is impossible not to worry. As we know, there is no shortage of things to worry about in our world. In spite of this, we can cultivate the ability to redirect worry energy into something more reparative through prayer.

Remember the formula I shared in the introduction:

Intention + language that matches your feeling states + visualization and somatic expression = positive change

If you swap out "intention" with worry—whatever you are brooding over—you've transformed a positive, co-creative spell into more of a curse. It's not a very compelling way to avoid whatever you are ruminating about. I'm not saying we should become paranoid about our thoughts—we don't need to be perfectionistic with this practice—but we can learn to catch when we may be in a worry spiral and bring a different process to it.

Someone who is well acquainted with worry is my good friend Alexa Wilding. Alexa is a writer, musician, and mother of twin boys, West and Lou. By the age of seven, Lou was already a two-time cancer survivor. Meanwhile, Alexa herself is a recent breast cancer survivor. These brave souls have faced intensely compounded fear and worry. I wanted to speak with her about how she has come to terms with living with extreme worry and the role prayer has played in her and her family's healing and recovery.

How did prayer support you during Lou's illness?
And what role did it play in your own bout with cancer?

Even though my family is mystically inclined, I never really subscribed to the teachings of the Serbian Orthodox church [in which I grew up]. Before crisis took over my life, prayer was a means to an end. It was only when the crises became untenable that my relationship to prayer changed, and I understood how to pray not for an outcome, but for the conditions—spiritually, emotionally, physically—to handle the tasks at hand. I learned to acknowledge I have no control. Through prayer, I was able to look my reality in the face, find the fuel to move through my reality, access joy, and still live.

The first time I ever really prayed was the second time Lou got cancer. It was a period of spiritual awakening. I felt abandoned, like I was on my own in the world. It changed my concept of god, like maybe I lost him. I think we pray to find god again. The night before Lou's brain surgery, I fell to my knees, hands together. It was a gut instinct, totally primal. "Please make the outcome positive," I prayed. "Please give me the strength and grace to move through the unknown." How do you even grapple with a moment like that? It's completely unnatural for a mother to not be able to help.

Around this time, I was introduced to Guru Ma and started a chanting and meditation practice. I started to build a "spiritual board of directors," which felt like a natural progression. It made me feel less alone. It helped me connect with more grace and courage.

How did your relationship to prayer evolve?

When I started studying shamanism and journeying, I discovered the practice of drumming. It was a way to work with prayer that felt more realistic for me. As someone with a music background who didn't feel safe in the world or in her body anymore, sitting in silence was intimidating. It was just too scary to be alone in silence with all the danger around. It's like asking a terrified, traumatized person to go sit in the middle of the freeway. So much reconnection to the body needs to happen, and I realized I just need to sit with myself.

The drum felt like an anchor.

Now I straddle two different traditions, shamanism and Buddhism. What they have in common is they help you reconnect to the body in a physical way—either by banging a drum or sitting with yourself. I'm finding new containers that speak to me and support my healing.

How do you hold the paradox of knowing that thoughts can influence reality, but also that it's impossible not to worry?

A lot of people don't want to face the fact that there may not be a good reason why a baby is born with a cancerous brain tumor and his twin brother isn't. I also don't get to know why I was diagnosed with cancer. There's always what we can't control. When you're hit with multiple crises, it can be very difficult to get out of the worry. Or you're always anticipating the next emergency. It can stall you from moving on from your life. How can I move forward when I'm the traffic cop waiting for the crash?

I am consumed on a daily basis, even unconsciously, by a story around dying. The medicine for how to not be consumed by fear and worry is to move forward in the knowing—and this is a choice—that everything is going to be okay. You can't ignore the worry, but you also can't let it rule every thought and every decision. The practice has become catching those fear-based thoughts, acknowledging the voice of worry, and moving forward. Plus, praying for the strength and compassion to know that I'm going to be okay. I'm going to be brave enough to know that everything is going to be okay, which is the fuel that is going to move me and my family forward.

Facing the kind of grim terror Alexa and her family has is a tall order. Yet, through the crisis she developed a practice that allowed her to make choices about what she thought and felt. It is these kinds of decisions that clear a path to move forward despite the fear, allowing us to choose to hope. These decisions show us a way out of the worry—and they chart a new course of being.

NEGATIVE SPEECH AND SUBCONSCIOUS SABOTEURS

Language is sound and vibration, and it extends to our thoughts and internal dialogues. Think of thoughts, speech, and beliefs as forms of energy—very powerful ones. The energetics of our internal language impact our emotional and physical health, and can subconsciously sabotage our true, heart-centered voice.

Trauma creates imprintings, or energetic imbalances in our subtle structures (our nadis and chakras, or the respective energetic channels and centers of our bodies), and eventually leads to physical symptomology, like gastrointestinal distress or migraines. If you are storing unresolved trauma as a result of an attachment injury, or a significant abandonment or betrayal in a moment of need, it will present somewhere in your body or in your environment—perhaps in the way you connect interpersonally with family or a romantic partner. As an integrative practitioner, I work to help people connect the dots between their history, their environment, their emotional and physical symptoms, and the challenges they are experiencing in their lives. Addressing our internal language is a natural complement to this process.

In my work as a therapist with complex trauma survivors, I often find that they have sustained injury to their self-concept and worldview due to experiencing harm over an extended period of time by someone who should have been in a caretaking position, such as an emotionally negligent parent, an unethical doctor, or an abusive romantic partner. When a person experiences prolonged harm, they will always *internalize* that harm in a subconscious attempt to resolve the trauma. This is the origin of much negative internal language. The more covert, or hidden, the harm, the greater the internalization of it, and the deeper that trauma and language will live in the body.

On a collective level, we've all internalized the beliefs and language of the dominant paradigm—women and systemically targeted populations most of all. So, this phenomenon is relevant to everyone.

Here's an example of the way subconscious saboteurs can present, and the role that transmuting this patterning can play in our prayer work. The following are variations on the kinds of statements that I regularly hear from my clients:

"I need things to be hard so I can feel competent."

"I need people to approve of me so I feel strong and safe."

"It's not safe for me to relax or love myself."

Our egos will usually lead us to attempt to externalize these internal problems. We strive to be super successful, or do whatever it takes to receive nonstop validation and praise, or feed an ongoing work addiction. Alternatively, we might internalize the harm we experienced by being intensely critical, cruel, withholding, and punitive with ourselves. However, in either case, it's never enough, leading us to only become more resentful, stuck, and exhausted. No amount of internal bullying or external achievement will compensate for being deprived of love and care. But it is possible to intercept this pattern of psychological self-harm and make a different choice with our internal language, which we can use to inform our prayers.

Here's how these aforementioned statements could be reframed, as we transform the downward spiral into a co-creative mantra:

"I'm open to trusting a new way of doing things that can be easy."

"I'm open to the possibility that being compassionate with myself is safe and beneficial."

"Real power means loving and caring for myself."

This reorientation away from inner bully to inner benevolence doesn't happen overnight. It takes consistent practice and refinement.

SACRED SOUND AND CYMATICS

"If we accept that sound is vibration and we know that vibration touches every part of our physical being, then we understand that sound is heard not only through our ears, but through every cell in our bodies."

—MITCHELL L. GAYNOR, MD, INTEGRATIVE ONCOLOGIST
AND AUTHOR OF *THE HEALING POWER OF SOUND*

The neuroscience on the benefits of prayer are compelling and provide valuable information for us. But that alone is not a complete picture of how prayer can impact our minds and bodies. The studies of cymatics, vibrational medicine, and subtle anatomy can teach us how we feel and function at an energetic level, and the role prayer has to play in this.

The ancient Egyptians understood the healing nature of sound very well. Their sophisticated acoustic healing technology can still be found in their enduring architecture and hieroglyphs. If you were to meditate inside the pyramids, you would notice the curious acoustics within these grand spaces. They are deathly quiet and reflect back any noises you make, however subtle, making them an ideal spot for toning or chanting.

During a past visit to the temple complex in Karnak, our Egyptian guide, Emil Shaker, invited us to place our ears next to a fallen obelisk. He pounded on it, and it reverberated with a deep *bong-g-g*. The ancient edifice wasn't solid, but hollow and alive inside. He said that the obelisks

Our Egyptologist guide, Emil Shaker, demonstrating the acoustics of a fallen obelisk at the temple complex in Karnak

were like tuning forks, each with its own unique pitch. There are count-less structures like this throughout Egypt, built to resonate with and amplify sound during ceremonies.

Sound has been used by healers of all backgrounds to channel spir-itual energy for thousands, if not tens of thousands, of years. This has ranged from Indian ragas, to Gregorian chants, to Sufi *sama*. *Om* is one of the oldest and most sacred sounds, originating in ancient India. In Sanskrit, it is noted as ॐ, ओम्, and is known as the primordial sound of the universe. This music is often either a form of prayer or a direct accompaniment to prayer.

> **"In the beginning was the Word, and the Word was with God, and the Word was God."**
>
> —JOHN 1:1, HOLY BIBLE (NEW INTERNATIONAL VERSION)

God is sound

Rebecca Kelly is a racial justice facilitator who creates soundscapes using electronic music and her voice. I asked her how she knows when she's tapping into her heart/source/highest self in the sounds she's cre-ating. "I've found that there is a truth that wants to come through all of us," she says. "And we each have our own access points for it. When I tune in to my heart, and the sounds come through that part of me, that feels like truth to me. It's not mental or intellectual, I'm following a feeling, and it can feel like 'wow' and not from an ego place, but a place of awe and wonder. It's happening to and through me. I have a lyric that goes, 'Every time there is a trade, any time that a choice is made, so don't be afraid to look inside and listen to your heart.' And we'd be best served by making decisions from our heart."

Rebecca shares that, in order to create, all she has to do is be open to listen and receive. In this work, she is in her highest self. She is the water element, merged with all the things that have come before her. "I'm in touch with my human ancestral line, and original ancestry, which are the elements: earth, air, fire, and water. That is how I feel connected to everything."

The Earth is bioelectric and has its own electromagnetic field and frequency, which measures at 7.83 hertz (Hz) and is known as the Schumann resonance. We've evolved to benefit from attuning to this frequency—it is good for us, and it is easier to do in nature, as the electromagnetic fields/EMFs (wavelengths of energy that resonate with other fields) of urban areas can create interference. Entrainment with the Schumann resonance adjusts our brain waves to somewhere between Alpha waves (8–12 Hz, very relaxed) and Theta (4–8 Hz, deepest relaxation). When we pray in nature—say, with a tree, or in a park—we are, in effect, entraining with the Earth's frequency, creating a resonance between us and the planet that is reflexively beneficial.

> **"There is an electrical current connecting the one who prays and the object of the prayer (which are the same)."**
>
> —THICH NHAT HANH

Sound healing has become very popular in recent years. Sound baths are incredibly relaxing and healing. After participating in one, most people awake from a deep savasana, perhaps experiencing insights and realizations. Listening to binaural sounds (as in gongs and drums) supports *entrainment*, in which one's brain waves synchronize and allow for deep meditation and relaxation. Sound baths can be potent occasions to both give and receive prayers.

Cymatics is the study of how wave phenomena, in the form of sound, organize matter. The term was coined in the 1960s by Dr. Hans Jenny, a Swiss physician who conducted hundreds of experiments and documented his findings in *Cymatics: A Study of Wave Phenomena and Vibration*—a fascinating book with many mind-bending pictures. In his experiments, Jenny placed substances (sand, fluid, and powder) on metal plates attached to an oscillator, which generated a wide range of sounds/vibrations. These sound vibrations then created different geometric arrangements that could be observed.

Jenny succeeded in showing what sound looks like and how it creates form from organized matter. His studies demonstrate that what appears to be solid form is actually created by an underlying vibration. **Sound—from instruments or our own voices—reorganizes matter and creates forms within us. When we speak, sing, and pray we create sacred geometries that reorganize matter internally and externally.**

Three Vibrational Vocabulary Words to Know

Frequency describes the number of waves that pass a fixed point in a set amount of time. The higher the frequency of matter, the less dense or more subtle the matter. All matter is vibration and therefore has frequency.

———————

Resonance is the process by which a field of a particular frequency or wavelength can transfer vibrational energy from one object to another.

———————

Harmonics are *"multiples of the fundamental frequency,"* represent-ing a state of coherence and balance.

—————

It is the frequency, and the ability for frequencies to oscillate in *resonance*, that determines whether a signal is healing or harm-ful, not the strength of the signal.

"Prayers increase spiritual velocity, which changes karma."

—TINA TURNER

Beginning in the 1990s, Dr. Masaru Emoto expanded on Jenny's ideas with his experiments, which have since been widely shared on social media, on how the molecular structure of water is impacted by human words, thoughts, sounds, and intentions. Emoto would expose water to kind and loving language, or classical music, which would result in beautiful, symmetrical water crystals resembling intricate snowflakes. Water exposed to fearful, discordant language would create "discon-nected, disfigured, and unpleasant physical molecular structures." He also studied water that emerged from pristine natural sources and con-taminated water, with similar results, and concluded that water from toxic sites could be revitalized when exposed to prayer and intention.

Emoto's work, though controversial to some, has been replicated in several instances with similar findings. These studies illustrate that: 1) water holds memory and 2) the molecular structure of water can be restructured by higher vibratory energy (thoughts, words, sounds, and intentions), which creates symmetry and balance in molecular structure, or by lower vibratory energy, which creates asymmetry and discordance in structure. Given that our bodies are mostly water, how water is charged is a consequential factor for us to consider in the sounds and energies we expose ourselves to. Do we charge our water bodies with criticism or compassion? What structures do those words create? Even repeating a single word like *openness* can be a mantra—or prayer—for positive restructuring.

Like Rebecca shared, the conditions under which we respond to sound are worth contemplation. Sound healing is of greater benefit when the body is in a relaxed, parasympathetic state. When our brain waves are slower, we can receive and connect with the sounds on a deeper level. We hear someone we love and trust differently than the way we hear someone we may not know. Likewise, perceiving our own voice holds a particular power. When your neurophysiology hears your own thoughts and voice, it's more powerful, there is a deeper recognition, and the brain invests more heavily in a resolution. This would explain why it is infinitely more useful to help a therapy client come to their own conclusion, in their own words, instead of superimposing my therapeutic opinion. Prayer can work similarly to psychotherapy, in that it can show us how to listen to and interpret our subconscious, and also speak to itself/ourselves, in its own language.

> *"Prayer, sitting with a picture of a holy being, singing to the Beloved—all of these are devotional meditative practices, the way of the heart. This outflowing of the heart toward the object of our devotion facilitates most other methods as well, through the flow of loving energy."*
>
> —RAM DASS

VIBRATIONAL MEDICINE, FLOWER ESSENCES, AND SUBTLE ANATOMY

We know that prayer has a significant impact on our physical bodies. I want us to consider the relationship between prayer and our subtle body and anatomy, because this association illustrates how prayer creates change within us. I've come to understand the subtle bodies and anatomy through my work with flower essences. These essences complement prayer work beautifully, as they both work on vibrational levels.

Flower essences, or remedies, are a type of plant and vibrational medicine. Vibrational medicine, also sometimes called subtle energy medicine, is a system of healing that engages the physical and, more essentially, the subtle anatomy of the body, to bring about greater states of balance. This creates the optimal state for health and healing. The concept of subtle energy can be found in virtually every medical and healing system around the world, outside of Western allopathic medicine, and the tenets of vibrational medicine are both contemporary and ancient. In the West African Ifa healing tradition, *ashé* refers to the life force or vital energy running through all things, living and inanimate. In Ayurveda, prana is the primordial energy of the universe that runs through all living beings. In Traditional Chinese Medicine (TCM), qi is the force that makes up and connects all life. Other forms of vibrational medicine include polarity therapy, reiki, and acupuncture.

A flower essence is an energetic or electromagnetic pattern of a particular plant form. It contains no active plant constituents, but rather an etheric imprint of the plant. Flower essences engage the subtle structures of our body: the nadis, meridians, chakras, extracellular matrix, cell salts, crystalline structures,* and energetic field around us. *Subtle* in this context doesn't mean faint or weak, but instead extremely fine and

---

* Crystalline structures include: cell salts, fatty tissues, lymph, red and white blood cells, and the pineal gland, and they work on sympathetic resonance, meaning they operate via attunement.

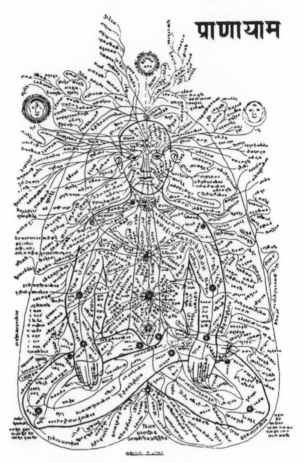

प्राणायाम

Subtle body and nadis, David V. Tansley, Thames & Hudson Ltd.

intelligent. Our subtle anatomy is closely informed by our unconscious and subconscious beliefs, thoughts, feelings, and behaviors (internal sound and vibration), as well as electromagnetic frequencies and energetic fields (external sound and vibration).

What does energetic mean?

Energetic refers to the subtle, vibrational, emotional, or bioelectric charge of something. Energetics are closely related to the idea of a *plant signature*, or the way in which a plant has evolved within its environment that points to its healing action. A state or condition to be addressed may also have energetics (e.g., a heavy, stagnant depression). An energetic signature is a numinous quality related to the plant's actions, which are similar to tissue states in Western herbalism: hot, cold, dry, damp, constriction, dispersion, and relaxation. There are a multitude of energetics that can be perceived by our subtle awareness, such as: upward-moving, downward-moving, heart-opening, grounding, and activating.

A main goal of vibrational medicine is to create opportunities for resonance, which brings the body into greater harmony, and thus healing. Physically, when something is in resonance, there is a coherence, which creates a positive attunement for a desired change. When something someone says "resonates" with us, we feel connected to it. It sparks a knowing within us that allows for greater awareness. As a flower essence therapist, when I call upon the flowers to help a client, I attempt to create an opportunity for resonance between the plant and the person. Flower essences serve as an attunement, an adjustment of the energy field. Sound and language can also serve as attunements, finely adjusting the subtle bodies and anatomy to experience a new harmonic.

One of the ways we can observe the way flower essences work is through their action on the extracellular matrix, a fascinating and recently discovered system within the body.

The Organ of Prayer—The Extracellular Matrix

As a healing practitioner fascinated by the energetic domain of the natural world, I continue to be led into increasingly subtler terrains in my work. Mental healthcare professionals in the West are primarily focused on the brain, but I am more drawn to the relationships (internal, interpersonal, and transpersonal), the environment, and the finer structures that inter- and intra-connect us. The extracellular matrix (ECM) comprises those physical structures that, I feel, interface most closely with the subtle anatomy of the body and connect us, energetically, to all life. It is also the system that intimately resonates, literally, with our prayers.

The ECM was discovered in the mid-1970s and is a dynamic, crystalline fluid system made up of fascia, blood plasma, lymph, cerebrospinal fluid, and interstitial fluid. The matrix occurs between the external membrane and the internal cells, and is protective and communicative in nature. According to herbalist Matthew Wood, "Each cell in the body is completely controlled by the ECM around it." No cell operates on its own and each is bound together in a communication network. The ECM "has a significant effect on determining the genetic expressivity of a cell." Therefore, the implications for how our environment—those energies we expose ourselves to, as well as our own inner thoughts and language—impacts genetic expression of disease states are significant.

The fascia and ECM *determine* the environment of every cell and therefore affect virtually every aspect of human physiology. Another way to understand the ECM is as a field where information is stored and in which it travels. This array of fluids and structures, which was previously considered inconsequential, possesses its own intelligence and control network. It is the interconnectedness of the field that influences the whole. And interestingly, the lymphatic system—which is both embedded within the ECM and also serves as a vehicle to transport it throughout the body—originates and ends in the heart, our deepest center of resonance.

Craniosacral therapy is a healing modality that expressly engages the ECM and holds a special understanding of it. Dr. Penelope McDonnell, ND, a naturopathic doctor and registered craniosacral therapist, shares that "due to the way it is structured, the ECM responds to the resonance of intention, thought, and visualization." She feels that, for these reasons, the ECM can be considered "the organ of prayer." The approach of craniosacral therapy is to engage, follow, and support the nervous system. This process leads to a stillness that's followed by a release (of memories and tension) and a reorganization. This whole progression mirrors the process of prayer. Dr. McDonnell emphasizes that the stillness "is the moment of shift, where the greatest healing happens. And the greater the stillness, the deeper the access to trauma, so the body can unwind and release at the deepest level."

The ECM is well suited to illustrate both the mechanical and vibrational nature of a system within the body. The Western scientific interpretation of the body is a collection of different forms working together as a machine. But even in this reductionist model, we are 70 percent water and 27.8 percent ECM. Even as proportionally dense beings, the fluidity of our form is obvious. Correspondingly, Newtonian science is mainly concerned with the level of form, but it doesn't account for space, which happens to make up 99.999 percent of our universe.

SPACE IS THE PLACE

The "finding" of the ECM, which isn't new at all, affirms the wisdom of many ancient and indigenous healing technologies. The ECM shows us that what is controlling the body's physical, emotional, electrical, and energetic functioning is less related to the physical cells and metabolic processes of the body and more related to the interstitial fluid and living matrix *between* physical cells and structures. It's the *space in between* that is playing a major role in our lives. And that space can be impacted not just by the physical influences on our bodies and environment, but by emotional and energetic forces as well, such as our thoughts, words, and prayers.

Sometimes, when we pray, it can feel like we are yelling into a void of nothingness, cold and detached. I want to suggest, here, that the space and spaciousness of prayer hold great power and purpose.

Space is the air element. It is the wind. To the Egyptians, Shu was the deity of air, and also of peace. To the Greeks, air was *aether*, the atmosphere above the clouds. Within the chakras, the air element governs the heart, the center of the entire chakra system, and is connected to the breath. In TCM, air is associated with metal, the foundation of interoceptive awareness. In the alchemical tradition, air represented the life force, and it was represented by the colors blue and white.

Even though the universe is overwhelmingly composed of space, humans are primarily focused on form and what we can physically measure, as opposed to nonphysical reality. Space is not empty, nothingness, meaningless. It is not static, but instead ripples like the surface of the sea. Action happens irrespective of distance (but not faster than the speed of light), and this is known as *nonlocality*. Space is the co-creative wheel of the seasons—it is the winter, the darkness, the new and black moon, the void.

Patti Smith describes the creative potential of the void as something we can animate, and as a place where we can station our energy, questions, and wishes as we engage with life and evolve.

When we pray, we have the opportunity to access memories and to re-narrate, repattern, and/or release them if we so choose. Memory doesn't function like a library, where you check out a book and put it back in the same place in your mind. Rather, it is accessed *within the spaces and transmutations inside the brain*, as "short-term memory is stored by chemical-electrical change in the neurons of the temporal lobes, and long-term memory is stored by an architectural change in the molecular shape of the neurons of the cerebral cortex." Memories are also stored within and reprocessed outside of the brain, throughout the body.

Just as with the living matrix, space is not an empty, purposeless place—it possesses its own awareness and possibility. It controls and connects the entire web of life. The intelligent living space between is connected to everything everywhere, and it is possible to access and positively influence this space. The point is not to extract something from this plane, but instead to see it as pure potentiality—a part of life with which we can be in reciprocal relationship.

THE UNCOMMON BOOK OF PRAYER

As a practitioner, I view the space between my client and me not as inert, but as a vital field. It's not me, or you, but us, together. It's the vesica piscis, where two spheres intersect to create a third element with its own alchemy. It manifests simply by coming together, and is strengthened by a shared intention. Here, a vessel is created, with its own knowing and intelligence, and the more you trust in this field, the greater the space you can hold for whatever needs to emerge.

PRAYER AND QUANTUM MECHANICS

The concepts of light, energy, and vibration—which are essential to our more nuanced understanding of prayer and its potential—don't fit neatly within a classical physics model. They can be more easily comprehended through quantum theory.

The rules of classical mechanics are firmly rooted in the Cartesian, mechanistic, and physical world. Under these premises, something is only real if one can physically observe and measure it. This model is concerned with the atomic level of life, and it does explain some of the world with accuracy. But contrary to popular (perhaps increasingly less popular) thought, Newtonian physics doesn't answer all the questions of the universe. It represents only an approximation of reality.

Quantum mechanics focuses on the subatomic level of reality, and is more concerned with light, energy, and the space of the universe. This model allows for the prediction of probability—it shows us what is possible, not what is absolute. But it does offer us more clues and considerations for understanding reality.

> "In the theory of relativity there is no unique absolute time, but instead each individual has his own personal measure of time that depends on where he is and how he is moving."
>
> —DR. STEPHEN HAWKING

A few main tenets of quantum theory are:

1) What we perceive as solid matter is actually highly complex, infinitely orchestrated energy fields, or vibration.

2) Light can be both a particle and a wave, meaning that something that has physical density to it can also be measured as vibratory energy. This means that matter/what we consider physical is, at the microcosmic level, as quantum physicist Dr. David Bohm says, "frozen light."*

3) Subatomic particles can be linked beyond time and space, and this phenomenon is known as *entanglement* or *nonlocality*.

4) Atomic particles behave differently depending on whether they are being observed and how the observation is taking place. This means the act of being observed changes the way particles function, a phenomenon now known as the *observer effect*. The very act of placing one's attention on something creates change, and you can expect a shift of some kind to occur.

At the level of quantum entanglement, all energy is interconnected in the field. One part of the hologram reflects and influences the whole, and there is no separation between points. This explains why a large and growing body of evidence shows that distant healing and intercessory prayer are effective for individuals irrespective of distance. Maharishi International University conducted a series of thirteen scientific studies and found that when just 1 percent of a population meditates

---

* Flower essences hold a special relationship to light. Each essence contains the energetic template of that plant, which is then overlaid on our crystalline matrix to bring in more light. Author and flower essence practitioner Julian Barnard writes that "Dr. [Edward] Bach's flower remedies are centrally concerned with bringing light to the light body," and that "the flower essence becomes a vehicle for preserving and transferring this light resonance to another person in another place."

or prays daily, the violent crime rate decreases and various societal factors improve. This has come to be known as the Maharishi Effect. These experiments have been conducted in a handful of other places, with similar outcomes.

PHYSICAL VERSUS COSMIC LAWS

Cosmic, or metaphysical, laws exist along the same lines as quantum theory. As our collective consciousness passed from intuitive to intellectual, our physical laws followed suit. This resulted in our contemporary scientific constructs, which were developed by humankind (predominately men) over the last 2,000 years. Much of this conception was crystallized during the seventeenth century, at which time science was heavily influenced by Christian doctrine and the belief that god created the world in a rational, monarchical way, according to absolute and immutable laws.

In contrast to these tangible laws of the world, cosmic laws govern our *meta*physical universe. This is another instructive model through which we can perceive reality. It embodies the rules of nature, which are ancient and timeless. While the Western worldview is validated by the physical, the indigenous worldview is validated by the metaphysical. Cosmic laws hold the secrets to the overlighting organization of the cosmos, which is based not on physical matter, but on energy, light, and vibration.

I am not pitting the physical against the ontological. Both orientations allow us to understand pieces of the universe. And at one point, they were not held in opposition, even by those most revered for their scientific minds. Most people aren't aware that Newton, like many men of the sciences during the Enlightenment, was heavily influenced by hermetics and alchemy. He believed that reductionistic and holistic theoretical models offer complementary, rather than conflicting, perspectives.

Nozze alchemiche tra Sole e Luna, Jaroš Griemiller, 1578

Rules for surviving and thriving on this planet on the physical level are changing very fast. However, I continually find comfort and guidance in the natural order of life. The universe is impersonal, functioning according to cosmic law, and there is an enduring constancy and infiniteness in these principles.

One reference that articulates the cosmic laws is the *Kybalion*, a text based on hermetic alchemy and ancient Egyptian wisdom. The principles herein may sound familiar, even if you have not read the text, as they are echoed throughout many ancient and indigenous philosophies. They explain the universe as an interconnected, vibrational, and rhythmic macrocosm. There are seven principles outlined in the *Kybalion*, and I want to highlight three:

The Principle of Vibration—"Nothing rests; everything moves, everything vibrates."

> While physical objects may appear solid, they are in fact vibrating very quickly. Everything has a vibratory field to it, including but not limited to: thoughts, memories, emotions, stones, plants, and places.

The Principle of Rhythm—"Everything flows, in and out; everything has its tides; all things rise and fall; the pendulum swing manifests in everything; rhythm compensates."

The Principle of Correspondence/Resonance/Attraction—"As above, so below. As within, so without."

Levels of the cosmos recapitulate themselves in relation to one another, and this correspondence always exists. Energy follows awareness. On a macro level, when individuals change, the whole planetary consciousness also evolves. We can think of prayer as a bridge between these cosmic principles and the change they can create in our lives.

"The human being is a house of prayer."

—HILDEGARD VON BINGEN

AFFIRMATIVE SPEECH AND THE LAW OF ATTRACTION

Applied to language, the Principle of Correspondence/Resonance/Attraction* provides guidance for subtle refinement in our thoughts, internal dialogue, and beliefs, which can create big shifts in our lives. All language—including what we think and say to ourselves—is vibration. All language is co-creative and can create either positive or negative outcomes. Energy follows attention, including thoughts and words. Affirmative speech is the Law of Attraction in action, and it illuminates how our affirmations and prayers become manifest.

---

* The Law of Attraction can become toxic when misapplied: in manifesting practices, overidentification with material gain, toxic positivity/denial of shadow, or if it's being used to blame people for their circumstances, e.g., criticizing someone for developing an illness, or experiencing an accident, as if it were a conscious choice.

We are constantly in conversation and co-creation with ourselves and our environment. While we can't control what is being manifested unconsciously, we *can* bring the less conscious into higher awareness, transmuting shadow into light. As Carl Jung said, "Until you make the unconscious conscious, it will direct your life and you will call it fate."

Spirit communicates with us through the subconscious and subjective, and through nature, with synchronicity and symbol. Spirit can work through you inasmuch as you are available and open to receive the insight through yourself. This requires us to validate our inner, subjective experience, as we challenge the limited ego mind, which is essentially the collective status quo.

Our subconscious mind plays a unique role in linking our conscious and unconscious, the thoughts, feelings, and memories outside of our conscious awareness. It liaises between our thoughts, internal dialogue, beliefs, and that which we are creating and attracting into our fields. It is constantly responding to and operating on subtle levels, even when we are asleep. It is the channel that links mind, body, and spirit.

Some features of the subconscious and conscious mind:

SUBCONSCIOUS MIND	CONSCIOUS MIND
Is literal, plays back what it receives automatically	Has the power of choice
Responds to internal and external stimuli, e.g., the words of ourselves and others	Has free will to direct or be directed

Responds to symbols, subliminal messaging, nature, art, ritual, music, the numinous, and subtle awareness	Responds to what is directly or plainly happening in our environment, and these responses can be modulated
Communicates with both the unconscious and conscious	Can create unconsciousness but can't access the unconscious
Stores memories of humankind and our ancestors	Is comprised of thoughts, memories, and emotions a person is aware of, which are associated with the ego
Influences the conscious in the form of memories, dreams (ones we can recall), visions, emotions, and psychosomatic symptomology	Can influence the subconscious through visualization, movement, various healing modalities, the arts, language, the natural world (e.g., plants and animals)
Attracts experiences based on our beliefs (e.g., If you continuously say "I need to find a partner," your subconscious will respond by creating more need/limitation.)	Directs experiences through conscious language, feeling, and behavior (e.g., "I am open to meeting a loving and supportive partner.")

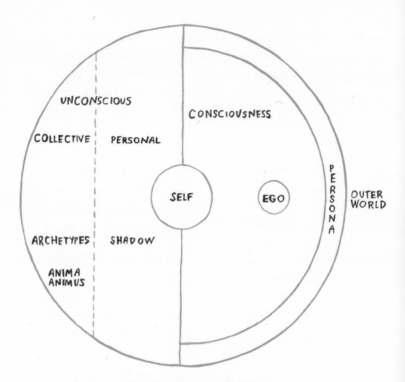

Jung's model of the psyche

The unconscious, subconscious, and conscious minds operate both individually and collectively. They all respond—but especially the sub-conscious and conscious—to repetition and store information more deeply the greater the emotional charge associated with it. This is why a consistent prayer practice will elicit greater change than one performed occasionally, and why engaging the visual and somatic expressions of your prayer will create a deeper resonance within yourself.

Several years ago, I was introduced to a book called *Conscious Language: The Logos of Now*, by Robert Tennyson Stevens. While this book is far from perfect, some ideas within it are quite brilliant and have deeply impacted the way I think about the relationship between thought, language, and reality.

Tennyson feels that, first and foremost, to apply conscious language effectively you need to:

1) speak what you choose

2) be first person, personal

3) be specific

4) be aligned in your feeling

Conscious Language Essentials

- *Want* is in the domain of lack/scarcity. Every time you say "I want" you are agreeing with wanting or not having. Start by changing any states of "wanting" (lacking) to "choosing" and "having."

- As a rule, avoid words that negate or cancel. These include: "but," "however," and any word that includes "not" (e.g., won't, don't, can't, isn't, etc.).

- Examples of limiting speech are: "I want," "I can't," "I need," "I don't know," "I don't understand," "I'm never."

- We give power to our experience through our attention (e.g., focusing on problems reveals problems; focusing on solutions brings solutions).

- Examples of affirmative speech are: "I choose," "I have," "I can," "I will," "I love," "I create," "I enjoy," "I empower myself," "I imagine," "I give myself permission to."

- "I" is right brain, and "am" is left brain. "I am" is whole brain. "I am" is our strongest statement of being.

- To neutralize a statement (your own or someone else's), you can use a statement like: "That has no power." (This is a nifty trick I use all the time!)

Start to notice how these limiting and affirmative statements feel in your body when you read and say them. These declarations will form the foundation for crafting your prayers, which we will begin to do in the next chapter.

Scarcity and lack statements are usually an internalization of some kind of oppression and are stored in the mind and body. These painful recitations are like neon arrows, pointing us toward places of incoherence and disconnection within ourselves. It takes practice, but as you build your awareness and intuition, you can learn to catch when you're repeating a limiting statement and reframe it. Then you can begin to feel and see the relationship between your words and what is coming into your field. You'll learn how to interpret and respond, instead of react. In this way, prayer work is a form of energy work, one that continuously shows me that we are the writers of our own stories. We are the artists as well as the artwork of our lives.

PRAYER AS A METHOD OF LIBERATION

What we believe plays a big role in how we feel and how we heal. However, most of our beliefs have been colonized, meaning they are the results of the cultural history of power dynamics in our society, rather than truths that come from within. This, of course, includes what we believe about healing and prayer. Some of the negative associations many of us hold about prayer mirror the self-limiting beliefs we are trying to heal and transcend, especially as they relate to personal agency, permission, change, and power. **I'm not anti-religion, but I am anti-oppression, and religions can be both helpful and harmful, depending on how they are practiced and spread. Regardless, I champion prayer itself as forever sacred—whatever sacred means for you.**

I've come to find that most of the misinformation, misinterpretation, and general negative connotations surrounding prayer can be traced back to the toxic masculine, white supremacy, and capitalism. And while reducing everything negative in our world to systemic domination can sometimes feel exhausting and overwrought, there is a veil to be pulled back on this subject that will reveal greater clarity, and, as a result, will further empower our prayer practices.

Throughout my spiritual and academic studies, I was forced to confront my own assumptions and biases around prayer. And my clinical assessment of my clients' feelings toward prayer as a healing practice has informed my personal experience. Though small in a global sense, I feel my clinical cross section of human responses to prayer is likely representative of a larger collective stance regarding our conditioning. Many of us feel prayer has been compromised by the powerful institutions that have claimed it as their own, sometimes to the exclusion of all others. Therefore, I feel it a beneficial exercise to look at why we feel ambivalence and resistance around prayer, because these feelings may reflect walls we don't need to live within. Once we get past these blocks, we are open to more possibility in our thoughts, words, actions, and prayer practices.

Before I started experimenting with the clinical application of secular prayer practices, I asked myself: Did I have permission to be counseling people on prayer? Was it ethical to confront their ambivalence and resistance? As a practitioner, naturally I respect people's beliefs, and if prayer isn't something you're into, I'm not going to push it. However, as I began introducing the idea, I noticed the response was mixed. I kept encountering the same resistances that seemed to stem from internalized oppression and, in some cases, religionized trauma.

Common responses to working with prayer:

"I had a bad experience with religion growing up."

"My relationship to [particular religion] was helpful in some ways, but also hurtful. I feel conflicted about working with a practice connected to that."

"I don't identify with what I was taught about prayer, or who we pray to."

"I don't know what I believe about prayer, but I'm scared I will do it wrong and something bad will happen."

I also encountered a lot of false assumptions or myths that people held regarding prayer. Such as:

One needs permission to pray.

Prayer is a passive, delusional, or disempowered practice.

You need to pray perfectly or not at all.

Prayer needs to be serious, scary, intimidating, and humorless.

You need to know exactly to whom/with whom you're praying.

Prayer must be connected to religion.

Prayer is "just asking for something."

These findings led me to wonder: What if many of us have gotten prayer wrong? What if its association with religion was optional? What if it is actually a safe, undervalued, more-powerful-than-I-assumed libera-tory practice? What is the cumulative impact of women and systemically targeted populations having been silenced, prohibited from, vilified within, and erased out of the literal and figurative canon of many inter-pretations of religious or prayer traditions? What if the resultant psychic wounding was an invitation to reapproach prayer, this time without harmful dogma?

Even today, women and LGBTQIA folks are still forbidden from ordination or top leadership positions within many—if not most—major religious affiliations. More orthodox branches of some religions often require total silence and subservience from these individuals. In some instances, women were and are forbidden from even talking with god. Even if you consider yourself nonreligious or atheist, this censorship and compliance has bled into the dominant culture, which has always required its women—and women of color most of all—to be obedient subordinates. What has *this* done to our relationship with prayer? To our perceptions of its purpose and power? To our connection with our voices and to self-silencing?

I observe that upon first introducing the idea of prayer as a healing practice, some of my conscientious clients are genuinely frightened. As a practitioner, this calls to mind the way women tend to fear their own power. Prayer and worship are very charged concepts, and they carry generations of both persecution and liberation within them. We have a subconscious awareness of prayer's potential, but also a conscious ambivalence or repudiation of it. Looking at bias, injustice, and challenging the status quo are not easy or comfortable—we're very much discouraged from doing this in our culture. In extreme instances, free and objective thinking are not tolerated, and this is the way cults, autocracies, and theocracies function. Confronting these biases and harmful norms, though, is what is required for us all to be free.

Religious freedom and secularism have their benefits. In their book *Scriptures, Shrines, Scapegoats, and World Politics: Religious Sources of Conflict and Cooperation in the Modern Era*, political scientists Zeev Maoz and Errol A. Henderson conducted a lengthy study to determine the relationship between religious freedom and quality of life. Their findings support that secularism is positively correlated with human security/quality of life. Further, they found that religious freedom had a "significant and positive effect on civil liberties and gender development . . . and allow[s] for more opportunities for women in health, education, and employment."* Restrictions on religious freedom were found to correlate to higher levels of religious persecution and violence. Even today, approximately 70 percent of the world's population is ruled by autocracies—governments like Russia, China, and North Korea. In autocratic countries like these, religious tolerance is generally very low, and there is also a profound lack of human rights. Religious tolerance is not only important for freedom of worship, but also for collective security and prosperity.

As I see it, those of us who have the luxury to challenge both internal and external constructs, and who have the opportunity to put that deconstruction into action, would do well to consider prayer as a liberatory practice. The embedded "isms" (racism, sexism, ableism, etc.) have

---

* The effect of religion on everyday life in a society depends on the degree to which people in that society are "religious" and "secularism is not necessarily the opposite of religious prevalence" (Maoz and Henderson).

created separation and self-silencing within each of us, and we must observe this internalization in order to exert more choice in our internal dialogue and prayers. The inner liberation of prayer can translate externally to greater justice and equity in our world.

Prayer should be healing and empowering. We can avoid injury in this practice by acknowledging that prayer is problematic when:

It is forced or required.

It reinforces blind faith, or belief that lacks accountability.

It reinforces cultural appropriation.

It is weaponized in order to guilt, shame, frighten, or punish.

It is weaponized in order to push personal politics or an agenda.

It reinforces oppression (bigotry, misogyny, racism, classism, Christian hegemony, etc.).

It is passive-aggressive.

It is used to bypass personal or governmental accountability.

It asserts dominance of any kind.

Prayer is a practice that belongs to all people, not just specific individuals, groups, or religions. It is not a locked door that some outside authority needs to give you the key for, but instead an open portal you can walk through, unafraid, of your own accord.

PRAYER IS MAGIC

As with the meaning of prayer, the definition of magic underwent seismic changes during the emergence of the dominant paradigm in Europe during the Middle Ages. Magic, along with folk wisdom, was determined to be a threat to social and economic control because it encouraged free, animistic thinking. This era was an inflection point in Europe, during which time and space were codified as linear and quantitative to secure their fixed relationship to capitalism and the regularization of labor practices.

People started distrusting nature at this time. We went from a state of balance and reciprocity with nature to fearing and needing to subjugate it. Likewise, people began to distrust magic because nature and magic are actually one and the same. Along with the feminine, magic was vilified and relegated to the domain of the make-believe. It was cast as crazy and evil, driven away from the enlightenment of the day and into the shadows.

For many traditions, however, the magic never died.

For leaders across religion and government, the impulse to obscure the narrative around magic was never about public safety. It was always about control. Honoring magic as nature and nature as magic reflects cosmic law and marks a reinstitution of the sacredness of all life. Magical principles are constant throughout the universe—only the terms attached to them in each epoch differ. Phenomena like electricity and atomic energy, once seen as sorcery and heretical, have always been here, regardless of whether people believed in these forces or were able to harness or measure them.

Magic, to me, is more of an orientation—a way to see, think, feel, know, and be. It is not something I use, control, or place needs or expectations on. Instead, it is something I observe and embody. To be magic is to be magnetic, in our subtle awareness, embracing our true nature, and undifferentiated from source, heart, spirit, and the divine. To be magic is to embody our dreams and desires—and work collaboratively and co-creatively toward greater collective change.

Learning to work magic is not about manipulating consciousness or matter. It is a process of repatterning ourselves in order to change the way we see, think, feel, know, and exist. It is the integration of the right and left brain—all our parts—as we embrace the intra-connection between the unconscious, subconscious, and conscious, as well as the inter-connection with the outer world. To work magic is to enact and embody Cosmic Law. To attract love, we must be love. To hold a vision of healing for another person is to hold that possibility in our own field. We can apply the way we visualize and speak (inner and outer sound and vibration), and how we pray, to this process of transmutation.

Magical Symbolism

The *I Ching*, sometimes referred to as the *Book of Changes*, is an oracle based on ancient Chinese wisdom. The first hexagram, or divination of six lines of text, is "Qia`n, the Creative." It is composed of all yang lines, which mean anything is possible. Paradoxically, this hexagram also reminds us that nothing can happen if you're trying too hard.

Six lines indicating the Creative, in the *I Ching*

This star hexagram corresponds to the magician in the tarot, and when drawn, reminds us that we have everything we need to create whatever we want. The magician works elementally (in league with earth, air, fire, and water) and *is the connection between* the physical and spiritual, the visible and invisible.

The Eye of Horus is an ancient Egyptian symbol of protection and magic. This image closely resembles a cross-section view of the pineal gland in the brain.

Magic is nature and nature is magic

Magic can be the mystical as well as the monotonous. It can be the ability to see beyond the material. Magic lies partially in our capacity to see, in the fullest sense of the word, or awaken our "starlight vision," as it is called by the author and ecofeminist Starhawk.

I honor all those who practice magic for good. Magic is a natural force, and just like anything that possesses power (e.g., knowledge, religion, wealth, status), it can be applied for either positive or negative effect. All intelligences at all levels have power and working magically comes with great responsibility. To work in accord with cosmic law is to always remember that the shifting of energy can create ripples of change beyond our comprehension and control, for "to light a candle is to cast a shadow."

Living magically actually just means living harmoniously, according to nature. It is to work with the knowledge that all life is organized, most essentially, at the levels of energy, light, and vibration. Just as vibration organizes matter to create form, we can organize our energy, directing it to influence ourselves and the fields around us. To me, working with prayer, energy, and magic are all the same thing, and while we have been gaslit into distrusting magic, there is nothing evil or bad about it. Prayer is magic, and it is completely natural.

> *"Prayer is my relationship with the unseen realms.*
> *It's how I co-create with them."*
>
> —JANE BELL

Questions to ponder:

What if prayer, magic, spells, rituals, affirmations, and wishes are all the same thing?

What is magic to you? How do you feel it and know it?

If you feel resistant to the idea of magic, what's behind that for you?

What if magic is not the same thing as madness?

What if magic is not something you needed to feel bad about or fear?

What if magic exists in the mundane as well as the mystical?

> *"If this practice is continued for long, divine contemplation will become a part of your nature. Once the habit is established, the future course of your life will be made quite easy."*
>
> —SRI ANANDAMAYI MA

PRAYER FOR PRESENCE INTERLUDE

I call upon this simple prayer when my monkey mind is running wild. If you are really in your head, this prayer pairs well with a few rounds of deep breathing and a quick grounding exercise. If something specific is pulling me out of presence, I may first say something to that consciousness like, "I hear you, but I'm going to take the next three minutes for myself. I will come back to you in a bit."

> I am here,
> I am clear,
> I am present.
> My awareness is oriented in the here and now.
> I access whatever support I need to fully arrive inside of myself.
> Anything that is pulling me out of presence floats away like
> bubbles.
> I breathe fully into myself.
> I relax into the Earth.
> I have no need to be in the past, or the future, just right here.
> I can be of the greatest service when I am fully present.
> I tap into my power best when I am fully present.
> I can access the fullest expression of myself and possibility in
> the presence of this moment.
> Thank you so much.

REPEAT 3X AS NEEDED.

III

Crafting Your Prayers

WHEN I WAS FIRST GUIDED TO CREATE A TEXT ON PRAYER,
I must admit I was a little daunted, and wondered if it was too audacious
a task. Part of my writing ritual included a prayer to help me trust that,
yes, I was indeed going to write about prayer—and that I would have
everything I needed to co-create and complete this assignment.

A prayer practice requires and encourages trust. Just as I must trust
that I am up for writing a book on prayer, you, too, can choose to believe
that you are worthy of asking for help, of having your prayers answered,
and of seeing your dreams realized. We can choose to believe that balance and healing on every level can be envisioned and enacted. Now
that we've explored the ancestral and multicultural context of prayer,
investigated the deeper potentials of it as a practice, and examined
some of the ways our beliefs and vision may have been clouded, we can
approach crafting our prayers from an empowered position.

As mentioned in Chapter II, I'm more drawn to the similarities
between various prayer practices than I am to their differences. In a
sense, within this and the next chapter, I am taking a syncretic approach
to create a new system of working with prayer—one that honors the

connections between the many definitions and schools of thought surrounding prayer.

As a flower essence therapist, I am always looking for opportunities for resonance in order to bring about healing and change in my clients. As we learned in the last chapter, flower essence therapy posits *resonance* as the vibrational frequency or energetic signature of a plant that creates a coherent state with a person, feeling state, or situation. Everything has a vibration—including language. So we can think of prayer as a methodology for finding language that vibrates at the frequency of ourselves and our intentions. Language refers not only to spoken word, but to internal talk and thoughts, too. Even if we are not conscious of it, we are always engaged in inner dialogue with ourselves, as well as other people and places.

For me, how we pray and how we heal have become increasingly intertwined. When we become more aware of our internal landscape, we can identify those places where we are out of balance or need help. Then we can begin to formulate more intentional statements that will become our prayers. This chapter will offer insights on how to enhance awareness of our inner selves, as we mine what lies beyond our fear-based, limited minds in order to plant seeds of real and deep change.

WELCOMING THE STILLNESS

Every time you pray, you are opening up a sacred space. What you create in this space is entirely up to you. I welcome opportunities to create from the void, from pure spaciousness. Remember that the void is not inert but intelligent (see page 65). Things need time and space to gestate. We have been programmed to be optimized. I encourage you instead to surrender any sense of urgency or perfectionism, and to simply *be* in the stillness with this practice.

Ancient Chinese proverb

Prayer can be called upon anytime, in any place. As prayer is co-creative and relational, I suggest making prayer part of your regular, consistent practice to fully connect with the magic of your intentional language. When I am working with a new flower essence client, I always

THE UNCOMMON BOOK OF PRAYER

recommend creating time and space to connect with the medicine, so they can truly feel it. It is the same with prayer. We can hear and receive best (within and without) when we are clear in the field, and not over-loaded with stimuli.

Regardless of what state I am in before prayer, I always start by welcoming the stillness around me and within me. Even if I am surrounded by chaos and distress, I want to get very quiet to allow the words to arise and flow through me. Accessing stillness may be challenging. You may feel a resistance to quieting the mind; it may be triggering for you. You may have so many external demands placed on you that creating a few minutes of quiet is difficult, or even unrealistic. Perhaps you will need to schedule time for your prayer practice. You might consider finding a place where you live, or in nature, where getting quiet feels easier. You could also try playing some ambient or meditative music in the background. Doing whatever you can to prioritize stillness in this process will be supportive to your prayer journey.

Rituals can also be helpful here. If I'm at home, I often start my prayer practice by sitting at my altar, where I have my books, journals, and sacred objects. I light a candle and do a brief grounding of my energy. That's it—very simple. The next chapter, Working with Prayer, covers rituals to accompany our prayers in more depth.

PSYCHIC HYGIENE AND PROTECTION

Psychic hygiene is a set of restorative practices you can implement to care for yourself, your energy field, your space, and all that you co-create. As a helper, psychic hygiene elevates the level of care that I offer my clients. It is foundational to my roles—counseling clients, showing up for my community, making medicine, writing, teaching, and facilitating—and also in my own personal healing work. The energetics we want to encourage here are: grounding, protection, clearing, and heart attachment to ourselves. Bringing these cosmic best practices into your prayer work enhances safety, integrity, and efficacy.

Part of the reason I pray with clients (with their permission) before every session is to set the space energetically and to provide a safe container for the work we will do. Working with people therapeutically involves more than just verbal processing and physical bodies interacting. It also significantly impacts our energy fields and subtle anatomy. Just as we would want to care for our physical body if training for a marathon, we also need to be caring for our minds, hearts, and spirits in our healing work. When we don't care for ourselves energetically, we are more prone to fatigue, burnout, sleep disturbance, accidents, and disease, and our subtle, extrasensory perception isn't as sharp.

However, when we are in an empowered state of caring for our whole selves, we are less vulnerable to stress. We are also less vulnerable to psychic intrusion and attack, which may come in the form of: thought forms and projections, emotional toxicity, psychic bonding, entities, and negative electromagnetic frequencies (EMFs).

Psychic hygiene is essential for activists and helpers of all kinds, and especially for the highly sensitive and empathic. Highly sensitive persons, or HSPs, have been shown to possess "sensory processing sensitivity," which is the heightened responsiveness of the central nervous system and deeper cognitive processing of physical, social, and emotional stimuli. For empaths with trauma histories, remember that your experiences, while negative, did bring you gifts of heightened psychic abilities. Our psychic hygiene practices, then, are invitations to reclaim the sensitivities we may have felt confused or embarrassed about in the past. Psychic hygiene offers us a chance to trust that our subtle sensory cognizance is not a weakness, but a strength.

Prayer can play an active role in your psychic health, and hygiene practices can enhance your prayer work. When we pray, we are opening a line of communication with the divine and the spirit world. We interface with unseen forces. Duality exists at all levels, even in the invisible realms. Interacting with the spiritual and psychic requires respect and an understanding that all is not "love and light"—there are shadow forces at play as well. When first cultivating your psychic ability, you may feel like a radio tuning into different channels, and not all of those channels are pleasant or relevant. We always want to be protective and thoughtful wherever we travel, both on the physical Earth and in the astral realms.

Everyone is worthy of protection. Anything you love or value deserves protection. To protect yourself is to value yourself. When you are protected, you can be more open to receive, you can be vulnerable, and you can stand in your truth and decisions. Being present is always more protected, while being distracted can be dangerous. At the same time, having too many boundaries can create blockages—it can direct light and life away from us. We want to have a balanced approach with protection as well.

Quick Prayer for Protection

This is adapted from an old Celtic incantation. It can be employed anytime you are feeling under psychic attack, and is best repeated three times as needed.

Any evil directed at me,
Is sent to the light three times three,
So mote it be,
In the name of the greatest goddess.

The following techniques work best alongside visualization. They require practice, and the more consistent time and energy you offer them, the more you will feel their beneficial effects.

PSYCHIC HYGIENE AND PROTECTIVE PRACTICES AND ALLIES

Grounding

Lower your gaze or close your eyes. Take some deep breaths into your belly. You can play soft music or nature sounds in the background if that is helpful. Feel your body making contact with the Earth. Breathe into that connection. As you experience feeling held by the Earth, sink in a little more. Imagine a cord emanating from your lower body/root chakra to the core of the Earth. This cord could be a rainbow, a tree trunk, or a beam of light. Feel this connection and breathe into it. When you are done, simply let the cord go.

Grounding helps us protect our energy fields and it enhances our stress responses. I begin every client session with this practice and may perform it myself several times a day.

Prayers for protection

Visualize an orb of light (any color) around you. I like to envision concentric orbs of black tourmaline, blue cobalt, rose quartz, and golden white light. Be sure to tuck the orb around your feet like a blanket, so it is connected with the Earth.

Herbalist Karen Rose feels a deep connection to her ancestors, who knew that protection came from beyond the physical realm and that "much, if not all, of their protection was spiritual protection." For daily protection, she recommends an affirmation such as, "I have nothing to fear. My ancestors and guardians go before me, making my way." Or "I am surrounded by infinite love, wisdom, and protection." This practice can include lighting a candle as you sit before your altar to share your thoughts and receive messages for the day. You can repeat the affirmations throughout the day whenever you need safety.

Ask for permission

I always ask for permission when calling a person's spirit and spirit team into a prayer or session, working with the land or a particular plant, or accessing the wisdom of a particular tradition (e.g., the wisdom of the sages of the *I Ching*).

Sacred space maintenance

Sacred spaces, altars, or temples are places of intention and remembrance. They may include sacred objects, books, stones, cards, incense, pictures of ancestors, and the like. You may have one or several in your living space. Attend to your altar space(s) in whatever way feels good to you. This maintenance does influence the energy and the efficacy of your practices. The more you charge and ground the energy in your altar areas, the more you can feel it and radiate it out into the world.

Infinity sign exercise

Visualize a silver infinity sign running between you and another person you may be working with or praying for. You are each in your own loop but are also connected. Keep the light running in the symbol as you do this exercise. This creates both a healthy connection and a boundary with another person. This works well in healing work or in any situation where you want to maintain your aura.

Journaling

Let your journal be a container for your inquiries, lists, curiosities, and wishes. You don't need to hold everything in your mind all the time. Be sure to note when things feel good and encouraging, as well as when things feel difficult. It's nice to have heartening reminders when we are feeling down. And as Erykah Badu said, "Spelling is a spell. Write it out."

Spend time in nature

Places with many trees, rock formations, and running water contain negative ions, which help us relax, lower our blood pressure, fight infection, and regulate our nervous systems. Just sitting or walking for a few minutes in a park can make a difference.

Maintain healthy boundaries

This can be tough for empaths and HSPs, who may be used to existing exclusively in helping mode. What people, places, and situations give you energy? Which ones take it away? Understand when you need to say no to honor your needs. In which areas or seasons of life can you enjoy greater work-life balance? Bach centaury essence is a good ally if you struggle with boundaries.

Aura clearing

You can visualize a shower of golden light washing your auric field. Or you may want to take an actual shower or bath. If taking a bath, you can use Epsom salt, which also contains negative ions, and has a drawing-out energetic. Visualize any energy that may be stuck to you or in your field flowing into the water and going down the drain.

Space clearing

Limit EMFs, which disturb our subtle energy fields and in turn disrupt our mood, energy, and sleep, among other things. Also limit screens and media. We haven't evolved to process all the information we are constantly bombarded with, and we need to be more discerning in what we expose ourselves to. Burn sustainably harvested red cedar, mugwort, lavender, or incense. You can use this to clear your office, home, or any sacred space.

Fill your cup

Rest, joy, play. Healing and prayer work can require a lot of energy. Be sure to encourage balance work through whatever helps you feel restored and revitalized.

Closing the circle

When we open up the field, circle, or portal to healing, we need to also remember to perform a closing. This can be achieved with a simple prayer such as, "Thank you so much for all those who assisted in this session/healing/ceremony. The circle is now closed."

Protective flower essences

Angelica, Pink Yarrow, Alaskan Essences Soul Support, Flower Essence Society Grounding Green Formula, Delta Gardens Protection Spray

Clearing flower essences

FES Yarrow Environmental Solution, Delta Gardens Clearing (tincture and spray), Alaskan Essences Purification Spray

Protective stones*

Black tourmaline, rose quartz, amethyst, obsidian (especially green and black varieties)

PRAYER FOR EMERGENCY PROTECTION

For when you feel unsafe, either physically or emotionally, or under psychic attack.

> Dear mother/father god, spirit, and universe,
> I call on the powers of my highest self, light, love, truth, nature, and healing.
> I call on all my angels, guides, and ancestors.
> I call on any past or future selves who are available to help me in this lifetime.
> I call on the Elementals—Earth, Air, Fire, and Water.
> I call on Archangel Michael, Brigid, Oshun, Quan Yin, Green Tara, the Virgin Mary, Mary Magdalene, Artemis, Lilith, Maat, Sekhmet, Isis, and Vishnu.
> Any negative entities or energies attempting to hook into my or my family's field: You are banished to the light and you have no power over me.
> Any energy cords attempting to hook into my field fall to the Earth and dissolve into light.
> Myself, my inner child, and my space are surrounded in divine love and protection.

---

* We can measure the ability of crystals and crystalline materials to generate electric charges and also transform resonant frequencies into other forms of light, electricity, or sound, and this effect is known as the *piezoelectric charge*.

> I am encircled in concentric orbs of rose quartz, gold, cobalt
>   blue, and black tourmaline.
> My energy field is clear, luminous, and sovereign.
> I am safe, protected, and all is well within and around me.
> Immediately and infinitely, my being is restored to perfect
>   balance.
> Immediately and infinitely, I perceive, know, receive, and allow
>   the maximum amount of healing to occur within me that is
>   in accordance with the highest good.
> Thank you so much to my spirit team and all those supporting me
>   in this lifetime, for your divine assistance and protection.
> With deepest gratitude, so be it.

PRAYING WITH ALL OUR PARTS

If we leave out what we think prayer "should" look like, can we come as we are to this practice? As a psychosomatic therapist, I utilize Focusing in my work with clients. Focusing is a "body-oriented process of self-awareness and emotional healing" that involves "having a conversation with your feelings, in which you do most of the listening." By cultivating our felt sense—a subtle somatic awareness that arises in real time—we can access deeper states of knowing and healing. Focusing helps us understand the parts of ourselves that might be more subconscious, and thus less integrated into the whole self. I liken Focusing to shining light on the rooms of your "house" with which you might not be very familiar. They might scare you. You may discover new rooms you didn't even know existed. Shining a light in these rooms encourages a different relationship with these parts of ourselves. As a response to trauma, there are parts of ourselves—of our inner children, our shad-

ows, our souls—that become crystallized. These parts don't need to be judged or abandoned, but rather acknowledged and integrated as valid pieces of our whole self.

When we experience pain, especially when we are young, parts of ourselves may get left behind, frozen in time, like a child hiding under a bed because they are frightened. These are the parts that need the most help, the most love. If we don't attend to them, they will often try to command our attention through interpersonal conflict, illness, destructive patterns, or self-sabotage. Welcome these parts into your prayers. They are already trying to speak to you, so give them a chance to share their truth.

Trauma survivors often assume that the worst is perpetually happening and forthcoming, when in fact it may have already occurred.* A consistent prayer practice can serve as a reminder to reorient oneself to the present moment. Prayer aids in separating what happened in the past from what is happening now, and also in seeing the possibilities that lie in the future.

My prayer practice evolved as a result of deep spiritual turmoil—this was my way in. During that acute period of healing, I was cycling through extreme states of hypervigilance and disassociation, and was experiencing intrusive thoughts, which are negative, repetitive ruminations that are connected to trauma. A "part" in my mind would replay experiences and exchanges from the past, sometimes hundreds of times a day. I could compartmentalize enough to function and work, but most of my energy went into managing my nervous system. Writing prayers was a way for me to invite a different relationship with the part of myself that was generating these thoughts. Through practice, I was able to reframe the intrusive thoughts so that I had some agency over them. What resulted were long, beautiful, sacred, and very healing prayers that I could call upon anytime I needed extra help.

In crafting prayers that feel real and true, one helpful place to start is by connecting with those energies deep inside of us. Healing occurs when we bring the unconscious into the light for transmutation. Much like gently catching the tail of a dream as we awaken so that we can observe it, we want to try to make contact with those parts or energies of ourselves that are just emerging, so that we can support them. Here is an exercise to try if you are curious to explore this for yourself.

---

* Sadly, some people are exposed to ongoing harm and danger, for instance in refugee populations, and this can be understood as Continuous Traumatic Stress Response or CTSR.

YOU BELONG HERE AND EVERYTHING YOU FEEL IS ALRIGHT

Focusing Exercise—
Making Contact

I first recommend safely accessing a sense of stillness before practicing this exercise. You get to decide what feels safe for you.

Step one) *Find a comfortable position seated or lying down. Close your eyes or set your gaze low. Take a few deep breaths and ground your energy.*

Step two) *Do a scan of your whole body and begin to notice any areas that want attention through a physical felt sensation. This could be something like a feeling of tension in the neck or a fullness in the belly.*

Step three) *Name whatever you are feeling. See if you can just notice what you're sensing, without judgment, and without going into a narrative about it. Take a few rounds of breath with this part. We're just making contact here, not going any further.*

Step four) *You can thank this part and let it know that you may be coming back to spend more time with it later.*

Step five) *Slowly begin to deepen your breath once again, feeling your connection to the Earth. Open your eyes and bring your awareness back to your space.*

Now you are ready to tap into your feeling states and deeper senses for your prayer.

ALIGNING WORDS WITH FEELING STATES AND TRUSTING YOUR SIXTH SENSE

Learning how to access language that aligns with your various feeling states is one of the most important tools for enlightened prayer work. Once you've found the words to express how you feel and what your intentions are, you will find that your prayers take on a deeper resonance and can instigate profound change.

Words are vibration. A harmonic vibration is one of coherent resonance, in which energies are oscillating in balance. A harmonic occurs when we speak from a place of truth. It doesn't matter whether we are speaking language authored by someone else or speaking words we've created ourselves—if we feel it, the coherency of that alignment creates a resonance of a higher order. We can also feel a lack of coherence (incoherence) or lack of congruence (incongruence) when we speak or hear words that don't feel true or real. When the words we speak are aligned with what we feel and believe, there is no dissonance, just pure harmony. I've come to understand and trust what is and what is not of coherence through my heart.

There are exquisite works of prayer, mantra, and poetry that I have found to be deeply healing. Others—not so much. I've learned to trust that I am allowed to discern what feels real and true *for me*. I'm also allowed to not know sometimes, and to leave space to come to a conscious assessment later. I am allowed to bow to the unknowns. Discernment is the ability to use both our mind and our heart in our choices. A prayer practice encourages and cultivates this skill. Trust that the words you need will come to you. Run the language through your heart and body, and notice how it feels from there. Imagine what shapes might be connected to your words.

11 Hz vibrating in water

Let's recall the scarcity and affirmative reframing statements from the last chapter.

Scarcity statements	Affirmative reframe statements
I want	I choose
I need	I invite
I wish	I allow
I can't	I can
I don't know	I know
I don't understand	I will
I should	I create
	I enjoy
	I love
	I have
	I AM

Can you feel the qualitative difference between "I want" and "I choose"? Do you feel how "I don't know" seems kind of stuck, like a dead end? Or, how does "I allow" feel in your body in comparison? Do you notice how "I allow" feels more open, like there is more movement there?

> **"Western science was founded on the idea that empathy, intuition, instinct, imagination, and other such experiences that are natural to the human species should not be trusted as a means for acquiring knowledge."**
>
> —MATTHEW WOOD

Like plant medicine, a prayer practice will enhance your inner knowing by way of your sixth sense, the domain of the imaginal realm. In addition to sound, sight, smell, touch, and taste, we are all gifted with extrasensory perception, also referred to as our sixth sense. In polyvagal theory, this refers to "the sense that allows us to become aware of our instinctual responses to our environment." Buddhism identifies six senses instead of five. The sixth sense is also known as *ayatana*, or "sense sphere." Within Taoism, the Egyptian mysteries, and numerous ancient healing traditions, proficiency of intuitive insight was the reason for study, and teachings were transmitted from the masters to students nonverbally—psychically and experientially. In the Druidic tradition, apprentices were trained to see, hear, feel, and think like the person they sought to heal.

I define our sixth sense as one or more of the following:

Clairvoyance—innate seeing

Clairaudience—innate hearing

Clairsentience—innate feeling

Clairgnosis—innate knowing

Clairalience—innate knowing through scent

In my experience, most people have one or two dominant types of sixth senses, but it is possible to cultivate all of them. These extrasensory abilities are not will-o'-the-wisp. They are hardwired into all humans and animals, too. These subtle senses have been conveniently villainized by the dominant paradigm. We are taught very early on that there are only five senses. This is done without any acknowledgment of the subtler elements of the sixth sense, as defined above. Reclaiming our psychic faculties is a radical remembrance of our whole, divine selves, and learning to trust in our words and what shifts in our world as a result of those words is just one of the powerful gifts of a regular prayer practice.

> **"Epistemecide is the killing of knowledge. It refers to the wiping out of ancient ways of knowing. . . . In the process of modernization, we have come to believe that anything that is not provable through the scientific method must be impossible. We have dismissed ancient ways of knowing because they seem irrational or naïve. We have placed our faith only in scientific materialism even though its certainties are continually unraveled."**
>
> —SEBENE SELASSIE

Healing work naturally attracts empaths. Empaths often, though not always, identify as trauma survivors. Survivors of complex trauma, especially emotional and narcissistic abuse, can be particularly sensitive to emotional and energetic stimuli, as the types of harm they have endured are profoundly intrapsychic. To survive their environments, those who have experienced CT needed to develop extremely attuned awareness and intuition. If you identify as a CT survivor, it can bring feelings of guilt, shame, and confusion. But when it comes to cultivating your extrasensory perception—and many aspects of healing work—I hope you are encouraged, as your history and experiences have helped you augment your emotional, energetic, and psychic faculties. I encourage you to learn how to trust your instincts, intuition, and sensitivities, and to see them not as liabilities that you need to override or deny, but as powerful abilities you can trust and celebrate.

Guidance from the Imaginal Realm

People most easily connect with their sixth sense in the imaginal realm. The imaginal realm is the place in our minds where reality is perceived by our imaginations. The imaginal is a liminal realm that links the visible with the invisible, the form with the formless, the physical with the spiritual. It is where we store insight, memories, and wisdom that we know on a soul level. It is the domain of the sixth sense or extrasensory perception, where our preverbal, trans-language cognizance lives. This realm intersects with the healing field and also exists beyond the constructs of time and space.

You could say that the imaginal realm is a domain of altered awareness, though, for me, access occurs when I am most embodied, not disembodied. When I am in my spiritual practice, I am in the imaginal realm. This is a prayerful space for me. As a plant medicine practitioner,

I can define plants with my five senses, but the way *I know and communicate with the plant world* is through this deeper awareness.

"Everything you can imagine is real."

—PABLO PICASSO

Wonder and awe are healing and very good for us to experience (e.g., they promote social consciousness and lower inflammation in the

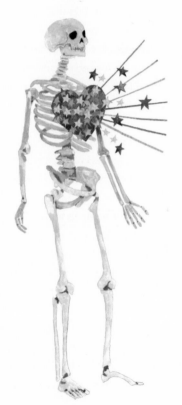

body). We cannot access these states by living in our left, rational brains. We must go beyond the cerebral. We must go beyond thinking at all. While you can't heal in the same environment that made you sick, you can use prayer to open yourself to new angles and solutions.

Sometimes, all we need is to be able to see what's really here—what's inside—and to remind ourselves of this. Creating coherent language is a way to signal to the self that the real work we are engaged in lies in the present. This pulls us away from an unhelpful historical narrative or repetitive thought loop that can set us out of balance.

How else can we crack ourselves open to the divine?

CALLING IN YOUR SPIRIT TEAM

I first reconnected with prayer through my teachers. Very early on I noticed that several of my teachers started our sessions with a prayer that called on a congregation of beings and asked them to be present throughout our session. We would pray that these ancestors and divine ones would surround us during the session, acting as resources and helping us maximize the time spent doing spiritual work for the greater good. Everyone has a spirit team. Your spirit team is made up of your angels, guides, ancestors, and all those who are supporting you in this life. It is a circle of benevolent beings and energies that may exist in physical form or beyond the physical plane. You may choose to ask permission to connect with your own spirit team. If you are praying for someone else, this is always recommended.

Ancestor veneration plays a significant role in traditional African religions. In indigenous African belief systems, the localized family unconscious, or Ajobi, is "guarded" or watched over by deceased ancestors, and family members may have a psychologically and spiritually dynamic relationship with these ancestors. In Yoruba tradition, when someone dies, a loved one will say "Odabo," which means "See you soon," because the ancestors will visit in dreams or visions and be attended to with prayers and offerings at an ancestral shrine.

I've found that, for those who were not raised in a tradition that discusses ancestors, there is often confusion about connecting with them. Much of Western culture doesn't give much thought to our elders or ancestors, unfortunately. However, our ancestors have much to teach us, and they are active members of our spirit teams. They live through us, and most of the time they want to be of service to us. We also have the opportunity to be of service to them, in the spirit world, through prayer.

Sometimes, trauma survivors will be rightfully ambivalent or resistant about connecting with their ancestors. There may be feelings of anger, betrayal, or fear that these spirits could be dangerous. If you feel unsure about how to connect with your ancestors, you may want to start off by asking to connect with your *benevolent ancestors*, or those who are concerned with your highest good.

Remember that healing is quantum: It travels into the past as well as the future. Healing yourself creates change within your ancestry, backward and forward, and being in your joy and your power sets your whole lineage free.

Often, people will come to me wanting a greater connection to their spirit guides. They believe in the spirit realm conceptually, but don't *feel* the presence of their spiritual team. Prayer is the first place I recommend going to facilitate a stronger connection with your spirit team, which is made up of beings that are here for your healing and evolution. You connect with your spirit team through the imaginal realm—your sixth sense. You may see, hear, or sense them. They may show up in dreams, through symbolism, or in nature. It's okay if you don't perceive them as clearly as a heavenly board of directors—they may not reveal themselves like that. The most important thing is to invite them in, and trust that they are here with you. You may want to make a list of who initially emerges in your spirit team, to keep track of who is there for you. The more you welcome them and open up that line of communication, the easier it will be for you to sense them.

> **"Be humble for you are made of earth.**
> **Be noble for you are made of stars."**
>
> —SERBIAN PROVERB

Your spirit team may include:

- **Angels and archangels**

- **Ancestors**

- **Archetypal energies: e.g., the feminine, the magician, the priestess**

- **Spirits from past and future lives**

- **Devas and nature spirits**

- **Plant spirits**

- **Animal spirits**

- **Elementals: the spirits of the earth, air, fire, and water**

- **Idea spirits: the spirit of a book you are writing or a dance you are choreographing (more on this in the next chapter)**

- **Healers and teachers**

- **Energetic spirit guides: e.g., the Spirit of Creativity, the Spirit of Love**

- **Enlightened beings: e.g., Christ, Buddha, the bodhisattvas**

- **Rays of color**

- **Saints**

- **Mother Earth**

- **Planets**

- **Stars and constellations**

- **Gods and goddesses**

Who's in your spirit team?

ACCESSING THE LANGUAGE FOR YOUR PRAYER

Some language is accessed by learning, conversing, traveling, and being inspired. Other times, the wisdom is all inside, a crystalized intelligence within us. There is nothing to be gained by seeking outside of ourselves—we just have to let it flow.

Sometimes the cosmic faucet is a font of ever-flowing energy; other times the spout runs dry. Some of us are more inclined toward verbal processing, so writing a prayer in a journal may feel natural. Other folks may want to explore movement, drawing, or other ways of accessing the creative writing process. Regardless of the factors that impact your ability to articulate your prayer, you can always set the intention for the words to emerge from your heart. Trust this process. Any place where you are feeling blocked contains a path to greater discovery.

Some Tips If You're Feeling Stuck
Try Breathwork

Breathwork is one of the most useful and accessible tools I've found for inviting change within oneself. Luckily, there are many ways to explore breathwork as a practice. You could start with a simple square breathing exercise: breathing in for four counts, holding for four, exhaling for four, holding for four. Repeat five times. Breathwork texts I love include: *The Power of Breathwork: Simple Practices to Promote Wellbeing* by Jennifer Patterson and *Breath: The New Science of a Lost Art* by James Nestor.

Get Off Social Media

While social media does have some benefits, by design it was created to keep us addicted and disempowered, stuck in social comparison and disconnected from source. In order to get present in your body and heart, and into the imaginal realm, you need to get away from social media. We are looking to access the inspired language of our hearts, not our egos. The capitalist model of consumption thrives on dissatisfaction—it trains us to look for external validation and solutions, when the real resolution lies within us. In fact, don't just get off social media—get off screens completely. Step away from your technology and get out of your head.

Get into Nature

Nature is healing and magical. Can you go for a walk near some trees? Sit in a park? Put your feet in a clean creek or ocean? Connecting with the frequency of the Earth and the elements is especially useful if you tend to get stuck in your own head.

Get Inspired

Prayers are not limited to spoken word. Throughout ancient history, they can be found in art, dance, and music. People may hold resistance to creating art—especially singing and dancing, perhaps because that level of embodiment feels uncomfortable or of little merit. But resistance is usually where things get interesting. What if you challenged the part of you that felt silly or uncomfortable moving and/or singing? Or if you are comfortable creating in this way—what if you let yourself really *go* there? Putting ourselves outside of our comfort zones and pushing our edges opens us to new neural activity and the mind-body connection. Where do you feel wonder and awe? How does the newness feel? What feels interesting, joyful, or expansive? Follow that energy.

Collaborate with a Friend

Perhaps you are both working through a similar process or care for the same issues. Crafting prayers with a friend is a beautiful and supportive option that can be mutually beneficial and lead to interesting outcomes. This works especially well if you're in the midst of a challenging time or situation. A friend may be able to help you arrive at language that may be submerged in the subconscious or that is too tricky to name. Also, when we work with another person, there is you, there is me, and there is the field, or new alchemy, that we are creating together. Prayer exists in this third field.

Consider Plants and Psychedelics

There are plenty of plants that encourage creative expression. A few of my favorites are:

Tulsi, *Ocimum tenuiflorum*. Drinking it as a tea is energizing and balancing.

Eyebright, *Euphrasia*, and celandine, *Chelidonium majus*, flower essences invite clarity in sight and higher communication.

Psilocybin from a trusted, sustainable source in microdoses. This invites expanded mental processes, psycho-spiritual breakthroughs, pleasure, and insights from other dimensions. There is a time and a place for psychedelics. Currently, they are being widely used to both great benefit and harm. Please bring deep respect for this type of medicine, the people and places it comes from, and your responsibility in taking it.

More information on plants and prayers will be discussed in the next chapter.

This is a great place to mention that prayer doesn't need to sound sanctimonious, ancient, or priestly! Ideally, prayer language should reflect your own unique voice—casual, fun, funny, or whatever feels like you. Think of the tone in which you communicate with a trusted friend and use that. You don't need to doubt or censor yourself. All you have to do is sound like you.

ELEMENTS OF PRAYER AND TEMPLATES

A mantra is a shorter prayer composed of a word or words, or even just a syllable such as om. One to three lines of text—that can be easily memorized—is a good length for a mantra.

See if you can isolate a negative thought or belief in your field. When I was in the throes of my acute healing period, I was working with a part of myself that believed I would be annihilated. This was the part of me that was hypervigilant and generating those grim repetitive

thoughts. So, I started with a mantra of "I choose to believe that it's possible for me to feel safe." Notice how I didn't go right to "I am safe." I didn't do this because that didn't feel real to me at that time. It wasn't aligned. I had to start with the affirmative language of "I choose." I said the mantra "I choose to believe that it's possible for me to feel safe" every time I caught myself having an intrusive thought. After a few months, I edited my mantra to "I allow myself to feel safe." Eventually, it felt aligned for me to say, "I am safe." I had to honor the reality of my feeling states and process to reach this prayer.

Bodhisattva Avalokitesvara, ninth century, India

You may choose to create a mantra that is not "I"-based. When I ritually clear my home, I like to say "Light, love, protection" over and over. If I'm on a prayer walk, I will rhythmically repeat "Love to . . ." and one by one list the names of all my loved ones. Another example of a time to use a mantra that is not "I"-based would be if someone you love is ill and you find yourself thinking of them often. You could, in those moments, say something like "My partner's health is restored to the highest level. Let their body and being return to balance."

Sometimes I will recite "Om mani padme hum," which is one of the most sacred mantras within Tibetan Buddhism. It translates to "Praise to the Jewel in the Lotus." Avalokitesvara is the "jewel," the bodhisattva of compassion. You can recite this prayer to offer compassion to all sentient beings.

Formula for a Short Prayer

Let's try out applying the prayer formula to create some language for a simple prayer. Remember, our formula is:

Intention + language that matches your feeling states + visualization and somatic expression = positive change

Let's say you wake up in the morning feeling grief for the Earth, helplessness, and fear for what's coming next. We can take this feeling state and bring it to our prayer practice.

Step one) *Jot down the feelings you have about the state you are experiencing in a couple sentences (e.g., "I feel grief for the Earth, like*

I'm not doing enough to make a difference, and I feel afraid of what's going to happen.")

Step two) *Decide on an intention around this feeling state, such as to feel more support or guidance around it. You could also ask how to release this energy. Or you could decide that you need to offer up this fear and grief to the Earth. A lot of times I will simply ask to be shown how to be with what is arising within me for the highest good.*

Step three) *As you clarify your intention, notice if any subtle sensations arise within you. The sensation might be something very simple, like a color or a faint feeling. We are allowing space for our sixth senses here. Make a note of anything supportive that emerges. It's okay if you don't notice anything at first—we will come back to this later.*

Step four) *Begin to formulate some language around what is arising. It's okay if what surfaces comes nonlinearly. Just write it down as it comes. You may arrive at language such as, "I ask for comfort and guidance for how to be with what I'm feeling. I release any of this sadness that isn't mine to hold. Please show me how to hold this in a way that will be for the highest good."*

Step five) *Say this language a few times and notice how you feel in your body. Does the prayer require further refinement? You can come back to this prayer throughout the day if you need more support.*

BASIC LONG-FORM PRAYER TEMPLATE

I consider shorter prayers (one to three sentences) to be more in-line with mantras. If you'd like more space for your prayer, I recommend considering this long-form template. These are longer prayers that you could opt to create for a more comprehensive process, or if you feel you need more language to express yourself. You can use the lines below each section to write out your own prayer language.

INTRODUCTION

I start off my prayers with "Dear mother/father god, spirit, and universe." To whom and what are you praying? Again, it's okay not to know the answer to this question right away. It's always fine to come back to any part of your prayer later on.

_____

_____

_____

CALL IN YOUR SPIRIT TEAM

Who's in your spirit team? My team is composed of my angels, guides, and ancestors. Yours might include plant or animal allies, goddesses or saints you have a connection to, Christ, Buddha, or another holy person, or those figures in your lineage. If you are praying for another being or group, it is appropriate to ask for permission (in this case) to connect with their souls and spirit teams as well (e.g., "I ask permission to connect with the souls of my biological family, along with their angels and guides, and all of our ancestors").

_____

_____

_____

BODY OF PRAYER

What is the intention of your prayer?

What is the purpose of your prayer?

Who are you praying for? Yourself? Others? The animals? The planet?

What are you praying for? Help? Strength? Guidance? Love?

I always include the phrase "I am surrounded by divine love and protection" in this part of the prayer.

_____

_____

_____

GRATITUDE

I always include an offering of thanks in my prayers (e.g., "Thank you so much for the opportunity to learn and integrate the teachings of this experience. Thank you to my spirit team for all your love and support. I am grateful to heal this karma").

_____

_____

_____

CLOSING

I like to say "May this be for the highest good of myself and for all. With deepest gratitude, so be it." You may wish to say something similar, adding a closing such as "amen," "namaste," "ashé," etc.

_____

_____

_____

Creating a Daily Mantra Exercise

This exercise assists in co-creating the kind of day you'd like to have, and enhances being states. Being states equate with "I am" statements. The ideal time for this exercise is in the morning, but it can be done anytime during the day. You may choose to use a pen and paper for this exercise, or to go without these tools once you've got the hang of it.

Step one) *Find your way to a comfortable position where you can be quiet for about five minutes.*

Step two) *Spend a couple minutes grounding (see exercise on page 14), or doing another breath or visualization practice of your choice that quiets the mind and brings you into your body.*

Step three) *Picture how you would like your day to look and arrive at two or three words or phrases to describe that (e.g., I am organized, I have enough time, I am connected to my breath).*

Step four) *Picture how this feels in your body and allow two or three words or phrases to describe that state (e.g., present, calm).*

Step five) *Allow two to three lines of "I am" language to emerge (e.g., I am still, I am clear, I am here).*

Step six) *Repeat the mantra a few times and let it land in your body. Edit if necessary.*

Step seven) *See if you can find times throughout the day to recite your mantra, and notice how it feels, especially any subtle shifts in perception.*

PERMISSION, POWER, PLEASURE, AND PRAYER

I set out to write a book on prayer and found that many of the themes within my personal and private practices intersected with prayer work. As Einstein said, "We cannot solve our problems with the same thinking that we used when we created them." We must be open to the process of evolution and transmutation to encourage resolution—within ourselves and our Earth. We must continually find ways to respond to the daily joys, frustrations, and challenges of life from the higher levels of ourselves. We must move from love and truth, instead of fear. Part of achieving this lies in the necessary and ongoing work of decolonizing our minds—challenging what we think we know (our perception) and the assumptions we hold about reality. We must remember that what we think we see or know may actually be only a layer and not the full picture. We all have to unpack and determine: What is the dominant worldview, and what is the truth? It is in this process of deprogramming and dismantling that I feel the interconnectedness of personal and collective liberation, and also find great hope for the future.

When I sit with people, especially women, and help them assess what it is they are seeking, I find that many of us are looking to feel better and to adjust our relationship to our personal power. This will inevitably lead us to explore the polarity of permission and power. Wherever we are subconsciously asking for permission, we are giving away our power. For example, we may feel resolute to be successful, but we are also waiting for an external force to give us permission to be in our power, thus allowing us to become successful. The current dominant culture is never going to give us (especially women, BIPOC, and LGBTQIA individuals, and systemically targeted populations) permission to be in our power, so what are we waiting for? What are we allowed

to feel and heal? How do we even define "better" and "power"? Who grants us permission for these desires—is that permission within ourselves, outside ourselves, or both? These are inquiries worth exploring if you are seeking truth within this terrain.

I assume some people will find what I am saying within this book to be sacrilegious. But that is one of the reasons I had to write it. We must not be scared to challenge existing power structures and empower ourselves. We must be allowed to define what is sacred to us. We must stop waiting for permission to unlock capabilities that are already intrinsic to each of us. We must reclaim our pleasure, power, and divinity. Prayer empowers us to do exactly that!

You don't need permission to pray. You don't need permission to define what is sacred for you. Nobody can tell you what your relationship to divinity looks like. You also don't need permission to feel good or experience pleasure. Some of us made agreements in childhood (or even many lifetimes ago) that feeling pleasure—feeling good—was bad. Let's say your intention for a prayer is to be at peace. What does peace look like for you? Can you feel it in your body? Can you challenge the parts of yourself that are resistant to feeling at peace? Does feeling at peace mean you're lazy, ungrateful, or unsafe? We all carry these inner double binds, but we also have the opportunity to unravel them.

> **"Pleasure is the point. Feeling good is not frivolous,**
> **it is freedom."**
>
> —adrienne maree brown,
> *PLEASURE ACTIVISM: THE POLITICS OF FEELING GOOD*

While we're on the juicy topic of permission, let's consider some areas where permission is advisable, and where you don't need permission.

This is an area where I encounter a lot of confusion with my clients, and I'd like to offer some guidance here.

Some examples where external permission is advisable:

> *When connecting with a wisdom tradition or teaching (especially one to which you do not have ancestral, familial, or cultural ties)*
>
> *When connecting with someone else's spirit*
>
> *When connecting with plants, animals, stones, or ancestors*
>
> *When taking anything from the Earth*
>
> *In situations involving physical or emotional intimacy (consent is also healthy here)*
>
> *When borrowing something from someone else*
>
> *When offering help or advice*

Some examples where you don't need external permission:

> *To be your own person*
>
> *To claim your soul work*
>
> *To state your needs, including taking care of yourself*
>
> *To validate your own experience*
>
> *To be in your power, success, and abundance*
>
> *To experience pleasure*
>
> *To be treated equitably*
>
> *To be loved without harm*
>
> *To leave a toxic relationship*
>
> *To feel safe*

May you give yourself full permission to feel awesome and be in your highest power!

PRAYING FROM THE HEART VERSUS PRAYING FROM THE EGO

As we approach this practice, I'm going to suggest that we pray from a conscious place. This is how we find our true voice. To do this, we can consider the difference between *praying from and for the heart and soul* and *praying from and for the ego*. Take, as an example, prayers for material goods. Praying for tools of survival comes from the heart and soul. But prayers for materialism and gratification come from a place of ego. If we pray from a place of striving to objectify ourselves in terms of money, power, pleasure, and status, this is all in service to the ego. (In Christianity, this is the true meaning of idol worship.)

I'm also going to challenge you to work toward praying from a truly empowered place—from the heart. Dream big and pray big. We don't need to be thinking small and scarce. We can't perpetually be focused only on ourselves and our problems. We must move out of the domain of self-interest and into the realm of community care and healing. Power corrupts and so does a sense of perceived powerlessness. As you pray, notice when you conceive of yourself as a victim, and challenge yourself to step into a more fearless, confident, embodied position. From this higher vantage, you can create great change not just in your own life, but in the world.

> **"I raise up my voice—not so I can shout but so that those without a voice can be heard."**
>
> —MALALA YOUSAFZAI

By paying attention to the language we reach for in prayer, we can encounter our victim consciousness, also sometimes referred to as the victim mentality. Victim consciousness is a domain of awareness wherein we have merged with the false belief that life is happening *to us*, as opposed to embracing a paradigm in which we are *co-creating with life*. This does not mean we don't acknowledge trauma and forces like systemic oppression. It means we admit these realities, while also recognizing that we have the ability to choose how to respond to our circumstances. It is natural to feel like a victim sometimes, and we may not always feel that we have a choice in how we get to respond. This is fair. But our thoughts and our language can be among the first places we implement gentle change. Victimization is real, but so is stepping out of victim consciousness and into our own power.

An interesting detail about trauma is that it is subjective. What is traumatic to one person may not be traumatic to another. This means that some part of the self (consciously or subconsciously) is choosing to have a response to a particular event or series of events. There is choice involved. **When we feel up for it—and you absolutely get to decide when and if that happens—you can challenge how you respond to what has hurt you in the past or is hurting you now.**

In my clinical experience, the people who bravely confront the parts of themselves that have been victimized, and build different relationships with these parts, are the folks who experience the most dramatic and sustainable healing. In complex trauma recovery, it is necessary to identify how and where we were victimized. As we progress in our recovery, it is equally vital to see how we are also a survivor, and eventually move on from being identified by our trauma and survivorship altogether. It is at that point that we can become whatever we choose. Many of us are making the shift from victimized child to empowered adult. White people, especially, must confront our inner victims (the places where we hold guilt, shame, and fragility) to be effective allies and accomplices for those who have been systemically marginalized, oppressed, and disenfranchised because of their race and/or ethnicity. This cosmic adjustment is happening on both individual and collective levels. Victim consciousness uses up a lot of energy—energy that could be going into more generative care for yourself and the world.

Victim consciousness is a voice, but it is not our soul's voice. It is not rooted in truth or love, but instead in fear and separation. It is internalized oppression. It is the space where we subconsciously collude with our self-limiting beliefs and thoughts. Using the power of prayer, we can see where we are attached to our inner victim, or making choices from our wounds. Prayer can show us where we are stuck—where we desire change but are unable to make it happen. If you remain committed to illuminating where this collusion with your inner victim occurs, I promise you will make inroads to greater peace within yourself.

With consciousness comes responsibility. A misapplication of victim consciousness is a form of spiritual bypassing.

This could manifest as:

- **Blaming people for their problems.**

- **Ignoring context and reinforcing "Everything happens for a reason."**

- **Invalidating someone's experience, or defining someone's experience for them.**

- Scapegoating or projecting to avoid taking accountability.

- Avoidance or denial of systemic factors of injury such as racism, sexism, ableism, and other types of oppression.

We all collapse into victimhood sometimes. It is an archetype that lives within the psyche of all humans. It is possible, if you can build the capacity to do so, to see where you are making a choice to stay, speak, or act in victim consciousness.

Some characteristics of victim and empowered consciousness include:

VICTIM CONSCIOUSNESS	EMPOWERED CONSCIOUSNESS
Archetype of the martyr, the "good girl"	Archetypes of the sun, moon, warrior, magician
Highly impressionable, trouble reality testing	Strong sense of morality, strong inner compass
Victimized child	Healthy, individuated adult
Fragility, self-pitying, trauma response	Resilience, strength, adaptive response to distress
Externally validated, need for external permission	Internally validated, gives self permission, inner authority

VICTIM CONSCIOUSNESS *(continued)*	EMPOWERED CONSCIOUSNESS *(continued)*
Extreme fear of failure, judgment, and rejection	Less oriented around fear, embraces knowing that one can handle whatever comes
Powerlessness, helplessness	Finds ways to creatively and dynamically transmute feelings of powerlessness and helplessness into something restorative and generative
Codependence, insecure or disorganized attachment, heart/source disconnection	Interdependent, secure attachment, heart/source in connection
Oriented around wounding, trauma, and negativity; low level of embodiment	Acknowledging trauma and wounding, and choosing to reorient around wellness and wholeness; high embodiment
Self-sabotage, sacrifice, loathing, and hatred	Self-confidence, trust, and love
Trouble accepting accountability, denial, projecting	Taking accountability, acceptance, knowing what is yours to heal

Attachment to emotional and physical pathology	Acknowledging emotional and physical pathology, and seeing the soul's potential for growth beyond that level of attachment
Overly concerned with self, own healing, filtering all life through own trauma, myopic, navel gazing	Concern for self is balanced with concern for community and the Earth, being able to see the bigger picture/longer game
Scarcity statements: I don't understand, I don't know what to do, I can't	Affirmative statements: I can, I will, I choose, I am, We can

This is very sensitive territory. We must honor ourselves and where we are in our process. Please be gentle with how you confront your inner victim. I also don't recommend pointing out the victim consciousness of others unless that person is asking for specific feedback. In your own prayer practice, examining victim consciousness can allow you to unlock a higher, more embodied state of self.

Questions to consider when confronting victim consciousness in your prayer practice:

When do you feel yourself veering into victim consciousness? (Feel free to reference the chart above if necessary.)

Where in your life do you feel that showing up?

What does your victim provide for you? E.g., safety, familiarity, control, etc.?

How would you like to embody more of an empowered consciousness in yourself and life? What would that look like?

Thinking back to scarcity and affirmative statements, where can you create language that is both aligned with your feeling state and is written from an empowered place?

How can you bring the energy of your internal healing out into the world? How can you be of service?

This exploration is one way to move out of the limited orientation of the self, away from the domain of "I" and into "we." We need access to all of our power at this time. We are the empowered ones we have been waiting for.

> **"The voice that tells us we are powerless is not our voice.**
> **We can shift our belief from 'I am powerless' to**
> **'I am powerful.' I will use my power for good, for all,**
> **for love, and for justice."**
>
> —SHARYN HOLMES

A place I have explored my own inner victim is with my impostor complex. An impostor complex, or impostor syndrome, is the inability to believe in yourself and your achievements. For instance, I know that

I am an author, but at the time of writing this, it is difficult for me to own my power as a writer. I am in the process of more fully coming into that power. Here is a prayer that I created for a prayer circle I did with a group of women, in which we facilitated a ceremony to offer up our imposter complexes to the fire.

PRAYER FOR THE BANISHMENT OF
MY IMPOSTOR COMPLEX

I am learning to have the kind of regard for myself that my loved ones have for me.

I fully embrace and embody my brilliance, radiance, and coolness.

I always remember that I am intelligent, and competent at many things.

I always remember that I am not a sacrifice but a gift to this world.

I know my worth.

The voices of those wishing me harm have no power over me.

The voices of patriarchy, capitalism, misogyny, and white supremacy have no power over me.

Any voice that requires or desires me to be: subservient, subordinate, fawning, less than, invisible, less bright or sparkly, dumb, meek, weak, dependent, afraid, unworthy, ashamed, guilty, or perfect is banished from my field.

Any codes, cords, agreements, or constructs I carry in my being related to these voices are cleared.

I'm ready to see where in my shadow this has been hiding.

I am finding a way to balance humility and brilliance.

I remember that rejection is protection.

I am in my discernment and know the difference between
unearned and constructive criticism.

I know when I need to be humble or accountable, and I love and
forgive myself when that happens.

Any unconstructive or unkind energy directed at me rolls off
my being like water rolls off an umbrella in the rain.

I allow myself to fully inhabit my life.

I allow myself to fully embody my body.

It is safe for me to be healthy, happy, successful, and in my power.

I need no one to give me permission to be healthy, happy,
successful, and in my power.

I gain nothing from keeping myself small and scared. That time
is over.

I need no one to affirm me to fully know my brilliance.

Though I lovingly receive love, praise, and care, I need no one to
tell me I'm special in order to treasure myself.

All need and attachment to external validation is released.

Anyone who doesn't honor my awesomeness is welcome to leave
my field, and I feel no sadness about this.

I am defined by my own heart light, beyond the bounds of social
comparison.

I am fully differentiated and individuated from the disempowered feminine.

This self-definition connects me to All That Is.

This is a reclamation of my light lineage, and now is our time
to shine.

> I call on the sword of truth to shear the imposter from my being.
>> I offer it to the fire. The winds carry any trace of it away for-
>> ever and the ashes from it nourish the Earth.
> I invite all my brothers, sisters, and soul people to join me in
>> getting this free with me!
> With deepest gratitude, so be it.

I'm pleased to share that after working with this prayer for several months, I changed the name of my inner Imposter to my inner Ambassador. She's both humble and savvy. She's not a fraud, but a well-respected diplomat who can liaise and discern between difficult personalities and situations. I feel more normalization around my imposter leanings, and I remember that it's okay to feel nervous and insecure sometimes. I can remember that creating contrast, while uncomfortable, is not the same as conflict, and I'm skilled enough to know the difference.

CLEARING SOUL CONTRACTS

Related to the ideas of karma and reincarnation are soul contracts, or soul agreements, which are commitments you made pre-birth with other souls, events, or conditions in order for your soul to learn, grow, and evolve. According to the idea of the Akasha, all our experiences are stored in the Akashic records, a kind of cosmic library. Some of these records exist in the form of contracts and vows that we made in other lifetimes to support our soul growth, but that have become outdated and are no longer serving us. For instance, you may have taken a vow of silence in a past life to receive protection, but presently you experience ongoing pain and conflict around self-silence. It's time to change it up.

Soul contracts have a repetitive quality. These situations arise again and again to show us what we need to learn in order to heal and evolve. Soul contracts are made unconsciously, but they play out in our conscious lives. Some soul contracts are pleasant, while others are painful, but they are all concerned with our growth. They may be revealed in: behaviors, thought patterns, intense relational dynamics, unhealthy attachments and addictions, obsessions, emotional blockages, and any problematic repetitive situation like legal troubles, money issues, physical injuries, or recurring accidents.

Some of us have chosen difficult karmas and soul lessons in this lifetime, but the good news is that while some contracts may feel interminable, they are not meant to last forever. When the work of the contract is completed, you can move on with your life. While it is not advisable to break soul contracts (as that goes against universal law), we always have the opportunity to clear these contracts to make space for higher consciousness. Prayer is a useful strategy to employ in this process. I always include the language, "If it is in-line with divine timing and in accordance with my soul's highest good, I complete and release this contract."

Here are some examples of contracts or vows that may be causing interference in your life and growth:

Vow of obedience

Vow of self-silence

Vow of self-sacrifice

Vow of poverty

Vow of isolation

Vow of self-punishment

Vow of abandonment

Vow of betrayal

Vow of disconnection from source/god/spirit/universe

Vow of suffering

Notice how you feel in your body when you read these. Do any pique your attention or six senses? You may choose to include language for clearing these vows and contracts in your prayers.

CLEARING SOUL CONTRACTS PRAYER

Dear mother/father god, spirit, and universe,

I call on the powers of my highest self, light, love, truth, nature, and healing.

I call on all my angels, guides, and ancestors.

Please show me what I need to perceive, see, feel, be, and allow me to clear any vow(s) of _____.

If it is in-line with divine timing and in accordance with my soul's highest good, I disavow any contracts, vows, oaths, spells, promises, or agreements that I ever made, unconsciously or consciously—the silent ones, the inherited ones, the ones accepted as my own—that conflict with my highest good or that have interfered with divine love and truth.

I clear all ties with everything that holds me down, back, and unable to see truth, whether by my own creation or by others lost in their separation.

Any and all soul contracts causing interference are cleared.

Any negative energies or entities related to these contracts are bound from doing further harm and are banished to the light.

Any judgment, shame, guilt, and fear related to these contracts
are cleared immediately from my subtle and physical body.

I release any contracts made with myself wherein I need external permission to feel happy, safe, in my power, and at peace.

I release any contracts made in an attempt to prove anything to
anyone.

I release any contracts made that ensured I would equate
healthy criticism and conflict with danger.

I release any contracts made in an attempt to reinforce fawning
and people-pleasing.

I release any contracts made that ensured I would equate people
disliking me with my worth.

I commit to use my superpowers for the love of all beings. I
return anything that no longer serves my higher or lower
selves with gratitude and consciousness.

I reclaim my right to choose how my story unfolds, creatively
and with divine protection. I give myself permission to
rewrite my own narrative as I see fit.

I release any contracts made anywhere that prohibit me from
dreaming, imagining, and visualizing infinite potentials.

Let the work needed to clear these contracts be complete and
the karma be resolved.

I am strong enough to handle what I need to remain accountable for, if any of these contracts are still existing.

I trust all of this is in accord with my highest good, and the highest good of all. I send this into the universe with the highest
blessings. With deepest gratitude, so be it.

Flower essences to complement this prayer:
pennyroyal, garlic, chaparral, silversword, teasel

PRAYERS AS COMMITMENTS

If you are seeking change in your life and in the world, you must be willing to make and handle change, which is easier said than done. My work is in service of cosmic balance, and this is where I feel great potential. To me, prayers as commitments speak to those areas where I am committed to growth and change—to putting my prayers into *action*. This action can take place in my own personal healing, in my allyship and accompliceship, and in my service as a helper to all sentient beings and the Earth. Of course, I am not doing any of this perfectly, but I commit to this work with my whole heart.

If collective, systemic change is something you're passionate about, you may want to consider:

What commitments do you want to make?

Where do you feel up for bringing your prayers into action?

What kind of support do you need to do this?

What changes are required to support your commitments?

What spheres of your life are impacted by your commitments: personal, professional, communal?

We're all making our way to the other side of the river. Unfortunately, many people are barely treading water and need help to get across. Others are having an easier time and have the resources to help offer safe passage. You get to decide what you're up for. Maybe it's being committed to forgiving yourself when you don't do something perfectly. Maybe you're ready to show up to a march or a monthly community meeting, to volunteer at a mutual aid network, to compost, or to stay open (instead of shutting down) during a challenging conversation with a loved one.

Our commitment language can be integrated into our prayers for greater potency and accountability. This offers a way to clarify what we are doing and how. When we bring our commitments and our prayers together, our agreements can become even more collaborative and dynamic.

As a therapist, I must contend with the reality that there are limits to the help I can offer people in such a challenging world. Many of us tend to blame and overpathologize ourselves and others for our struggles, instead of looking at the pathogenic systems of bias in which we operate. I also find that if we are not clear in our commitments, the pressure of constantly needing to do the work and do better can morph into ethical perfectionism, and an attempt to defend one's virtue, which seems more stifling than productive.

Early in our work together, my teacher Jane would say that nothing would change until white people were willing to give up their privilege. This was before I had any concept of my privilege or social justice—it took me years to fully grok this message. More recently, I was part of an antiracist accountability group for white-identifying mental health practitioners. One of our group assignments was to watch a talk given by teacher and activist Bettina L. Love on her book, *We Want to Do More Than Survive*. In this video, Bettina urges us to courageously contemplate:

> *What skin are you going to put in the game? Why do we think we don't have to give anything up?*

This led me to wonder:

> *Why do we think we can have it any way we want?*

> *Why do we think we can just get, get, get without being in some kind of reciprocity?*

It doesn't work like that.

Dismantling oppressive systems requires much external, structural work that is also highly dependent on inner work. You have to love yourself to do this work. You have to be able to forgive yourself for messing up, as you inevitably will, and keep trying your best. You can't be an effective changemaker without self-love. How will you work through the inevitable fragility, guilt, and shame that come with putting skin in this game? There's no resilience to tap into if you're not caring for yourself.

Solidarity arises out of mutuality. Interconnectedness is a social, natural, and cosmic axiom. We can align our words with our actions. Words carry great weight, but it's also true that actions speak louder than words. All talk with no action is another form of sabotage.

When things feel hard, when I go into doubt or my victim consciousness, I get to be in my agency and trust in my commitments and the commitments of my community. I get to turn to prayer, and have faith in the language I've created and its profound changemaking power. I turn to the words that have arisen within me through an embodied, heart-centered, conscious process. What higher order of guidance is there than that?

Just as the solutions for the many problems we face today cannot be brought about from the same consciousness that created them, we cannot arrive at creative solutions for ourselves with the same limitations in our minds, bodies, and spirits. How are you committed to your growth? Often, growth is accompanied by discomfort. We should expect to experience grief, despair, shame, and guilt, as they are part of transformation. We need to have inner transformative processes to work through these feeling states. Prayer as a practice of inquiry and discovery can be a useful tool in this endeavor. When we find the aligned language within us, our prayers can offer direction and strength in work that is bigger than our fear—that's bigger, even, than ourselves.

CULTURAL APPROPRIATION OF PRAYER PRACTICES

As you are selecting language for your prayer, remember to be sensitive to cultural and spiritual appropriation. It is a fine line between honoring a tradition and appropriating from it. Before you take something on from another tradition, thoughtfully consider how and why you are doing so. When you are applying prayer as a liberatory, healing practice, you may fear doing harm. Acknowledging the real power behind this practice doesn't need to evoke fear, but it is a good idea to be respectful of what it means to incorporate practices that are not your own. One way to achieve this is by being mindful of cultural appropriation, which is the "unacknowledged or inappropriate adoption of the customs, practices, ideas, etc., of one people or society by members of another and typically more dominant people or society."

We can also avoid trespassing within *closed practices*, which are those rituals that you must be a physical descendent of, or formally initiated into, to be part of (e.g., Jewish mysticism, otherwise known as Kabbala, or certain Native American indigenous customs). Not all wisdom is meant to be disseminated to the general public.

> **"First, they came to take our land and water, then our fish and game. Now they want our religions as well. . . .**
> **This is just another in a very long series of thefts from Indian people, and in some ways, this is the worst one yet."**
> —TULALIP ELDER AND FISHING RIGHTS ACTIVIST, JANET MCCLOUD

How can we be appreciative of other cultures and traditions without being appropriative?

- Do your research: Where does a particular tradition come from? What is the history and cultural significance surrounding this practice? Who are the physical descendants of this lineage? Do you have any ancestry related to it? Do you need permission from someone inside this group to participate in these practices?

- Reverend Myke Johnson wants us not to see Native American Indians as "spiritual surrogates," or this projection of a mystical or spiritual "other" who can serve as a means to salvation or spiritual awakening. Instead, she suggests doing one's own spiritual work and connecting with source on your own (e.g., paying attention as you go on a walk in the woods). Discover your own ancestors, rituals, and traditions—even if they are connected to the dominant paradigm and you feel conflicted about this. There is sacred meaning there, even if the history of your tradition may be complex or challenging.

- If using sacred objects, consider their origin. Prayer flags aren't just cute, aesthetic decorations—they hold tremendous spiritual significance to Buddhists. Plants such as white sage and palo santo have been overharvested and used outside of their sacred purpose. There are many other plants that can be burned that are neither endangered nor exclusive to indigenous groups. Two that I love are ethically harvested cedar root and mugwort.

- Listen to and elevate the voices and experiences of members of a particular group.

- **If engaging with a particular ritual like a vision quest or sweat lodge, consider who is leading the ceremony, where the money is going, if it is supporting the group it's related to, or if it is contributing to erasure.**

- **If appropriate, ask permission to engage in a particular practice.**

- **Always provide credit and offer compensation when applicable.**

DIVINE TIMING

Considering when to craft and offer our prayers provides an opportunity to root our prayer practices in our lives in authentic ways. I pray every day, usually in the morning, and sometimes only for a few minutes. I also set aside more time for greater stillness and longer, more in-depth prayers around what I think of as *my* holy days: solstices, equinoxes, birthdays, death days, and anniversaries that are special to me. Just remember: You don't have to pray according to anyone else's calendar. You also don't have to pray according to a perfectionistic, ideal timeline. As I wrote earlier, prayer is magic and magic is natural. Nature doesn't rush. We, too, need to learn how to let it all unfold organically.

Our modern-day Gregorian calendar is based on the sun and it runs most of the world's economies. It was created by Pope Gregory XIII in the sixteenth century and is firmly rooted in Renaissance Christian traditions in Western Europe. Prehistorically, most of the world's calendars—and there were many—were organized around the moon. Most Christian holidays (e.g., Christmas and Easter) were deliberately tied to the timing of pagan and pre-Abrahamic religious holy days associated with the solstices and equinoxes—days honoring the organic cycles of the Earth. In *The Bloom Book*, I discuss some of the traits of sun times (associated with the

THE HOURS THAT FLOWERS OPEN.

Linnaeus' floral clock, Getty

masculine/patriarchy) and moon times (feminine/matriarchy). The holiness of Sundays in some traditions—like Christianity—may resonate with you, or it may not. But regardless of whether days designated by others feel especially resonant for you, prayer can absolutely be part of a practice to honor the days and times that feel holy *to you*.

Many of us have often felt misaligned with the sun calendar we use today. The sun times we have been living in are typified by a scarcity model: an attachment to productivity, grind culture, optimization, busyness, and a preoccupation with the future—all of which are also facets of capitalism.

The dominant culture assumes the concept of time to be universal; however, many indigenous languages underscore very different understandings of time, and therefore space. These understandings create distinct metaphysical clues for us. For instance, the Hopi language famously contains no words or expressions that refer directly to time—they have no past, present, or future tenses at all. Rather, the language exists in a sort of omnipresent state of constant beingness.

What if time were not a future-oriented straight line?

What if it were a circle with no beginning and no end, only eternal presence?

What if time had nothing to do with "enoughness"?

These are the sorts of questions a more lunar-oriented sense of time invites.

You might ask yourself: Is there a time of day when I feel a deeper connection to my spiritual self? The answer to that question might cue a great time to begin developing your prayer practice. This is an important part of many prayer traditions. For instance, some traditions encourage prayer at certain times throughout the day, for example, the prayers of Salah in Islam at sunrise and sunset. Within the Celtic Scottish tradition, making "petitions" or offerings at holy wells is served by particular times of day as well. "The most powerful times to approach a well are sunrise and sunset, when the first rays hit the water. It is an old magical axiom that where fire and water come together, there is the highest potential for magic."

Humans have always prayed with the natural rhythms of the sun, moon, planets, and stars. The word *solstice* comes from the Latin words for sun, *sol* and *sistere*, which means to stay still. These are the holy days of the ancestral realm, when humans worshiped nature and the Earth. Solstices mark those points in the year when the light is the nearest (summer solstice in the northern hemisphere) and farthest (winter solstice in the southern hemisphere) from Earth. Equinoxes are the midpoints between the solstices. These sacred days herald coming seasons in the wheel of life. These quarter crossings illuminate those times during the year when the cosmic curtain between the physical and spirit world is attenuated. The solstices were very important to the Mayan people, who constructed their cities and architecture to perfectly align with the sun and its movements throughout the year.

Nanã Buruku, an òrìṣà of Candomblé. Nanã Buruku is the supreme feminine deity in the Yoruba tradition. She is represented by the dark moon. Nanã helps us to remember to go inward, to make space, so that wisdom can emerge from within.

Along with the solstices, equinoxes, and lunar times, certain astrological transits can be auspicious occasions for prayer work. To tap into these powerful times, it can be helpful to know the basics of your natal chart. What are your sun, moon, and rising signs? It is said in the Vedic astrological tradition, for example, that prayers offered during the windows of eclipses amplify the potency of a prayer tenfold.

What are the days that feel holy to you? It could be birthdays, death days, anniversaries, holidays, or days that mark important turning points in your life, like getting sober or leaving a toxic relationship. We subconsciously hold the imprints of important days within us. You may notice synchronicities happening on the anniversary of the death of a loved one, for instance. If you can be open to the symbolism of these experiences, the signs may have more to share with you, providing inspiration for your prayers.

Threshold experiences like births, deaths, near-death experiences, spiritual crises, visitations, dark nights of the soul, and mystical experiences can create openings for light, shadow, and information to pass through. I've learned that connection with the otherworld happens in slivers, little revelations of the mysterious inner/outer workings of things. There is usually a brief period of time directly preceding and following an event of this nature when the clouds part for a few moments, offering a glimpse of something beyond.

Timing tip: Remember that your prayers are living documents. You can change them as you need to. You're always allowed to change your mind—that can actually be a good thing!

Just as we can be intentional with when we pray, we must be open to the great mystery of divine timing. Paradoxically, in many spiritual practices, we are asked to be both clear and detached from outcomes. As the high priestess card in the tarot teaches us, sacred knowledge is both implicit and explicit. It can only be revealed in its own time, when we are ready to see beyond the material realm. We may only perceive parts of the riddle here in the third dimension, but there is always a divine plan playing out beyond our knowing. This approach to prayer work will definitely grow your capacity to trust yourself and the infinite wisdom of the universe.

SAMPLE PRAYERS

Below are some sample prayers you can reference. You are encouraged to edit them to suit your needs. In this age of never-ending content, appropriation and plagiarism are widespread. My prayers aren't propri-etary, but they are creations that came through me. I ask, respectfully, that you remain accountable if you share them, and remember to offer appropriate credit where it is due. Please note that the time/tense words I have chosen for this text are reflective of where I am in my process with some of these subjects. Be sure to check in with yourself before praying to find the right words for you.

I recommend invoking these prayers while seated, or lying down, with a soft gaze. Alternatively, you can also record yourself reciting prayers and play the sound back to yourself. Remember to take a few deep breaths to center yourself. Sometimes closing our eyes and breath-ing can bring up uncomfortable emotions. See if you can allow this practice to build your capacity to tolerate any distress that arises from doing so. Remember always that you get to decide what feels safe for you. This is a practice. The more you commit to doing it, the greater the results you will see and feel.

PRAYER FOR WHEN YOUR ANIMAL IS SICK

Dear mother/father god, spirit, and universe,

I ask permission to call on the powers of my highest self, light, love, truth, nature, and healing.

I ask permission to call on the spirit of my/the animal [animal's name] and their angels and guides.

[animal's name] is surrounded in divine love and protection.

[animal's name] is purified and blessed.

All healing energies available to assist them both internally and externally are activated immediately.

Any blockages to maximum healing are cleared immediately.

I trust in the intelligence of [animal's name]'s body and being.

I trust in [animal's name]'s ability to heal and recover fully.

I trust in [animal's name]'s ability to come back into balance.

I visualize an orb of cobalt blue light around them, bringing them back into perfect balance.

Please help me to be fully resourced to be of service to [animal's name] at this time.

Thank you so much for all the love and support.

With deepest gratitude, so be it.

Flower essences to complement this prayer:

Five-Flower Formula (which is also completely safe for animals)

PRAYER FOR SAYING GOODBYE TO
A FRIEND OR LOVER

Dear mother/father god, spirit, and universe,

I ask permission to call on the powers of my highest self, light, love, truth, nature, and healing.

I ask permission to call on the spirit of _____ and their angels and guides.

I declare from my full self to all who surround me that I acknowledge the depth of my sorrow in our relationship coming to an end.

In this moment, I feel heartbroken, abandoned [additional emotions]. I am filled with deep grief.

For everything I didn't see clearly, any projections or unfair expectations, I am sorry.

I ask for forgiveness for any harm I knowingly or unknowingly perpetrated in our relationship.

I wish _____ the highest healing.

Please help me heal the part of myself that believes this loss is my fault, is a result of my badness, and is the universe punishing me.

Please help me reach a place of acceptance and truth in this dissolution. Help me know what is mine to heal, and what is ready to be released.

Any places where my energy is attempting to hook into your field are returned to me.

Any places where your energy is attempting to hook into my field are returned to you. And all is surrounded in light.

All cords between us are released immediately and in all lifetimes.

We have concluded the work we agreed to take on together,
and all karma between us is cleared, immediately and in all
lifetimes.
Let there be peace between us.
I am grateful for the time we got to spend together. For all the
laughter, love, and discovery. I choose to remember our time
together in gratitude.
Thank you so much for the lessons I am learning about abandonment, betrayal, and loss.
Thank you to all of my spirit team for giving me the support I
need to heal through this experience, to learn and integrate
all lessons to the best of my ability, for the highest good of all.
With deepest gratitude, so be it.

Flower essences to complement this prayer:
skullcap, teasel, bleeding heart

PRAYER FOR COMPLICATED LOSS

Prayer can be especially useful for high-conflict relationships, or those
relationships in which differences are unreconciled. Prayer can be a
means for bringing these situations into greater peace and resolution,
and this prayer is in service of supporting you to that end.

Dear mother/father god, spirit, and universe,
I ask permission to call on the powers of my highest self, light,
shadow, love, truth, nature, and healing.
I ask permission to call on the spirit of _____, along with
their angels and guides, our ancestors, and all those who
support our work together.

I wish you the highest healing in your soul's journey.

I call on the light to surround our/my entire family and lineage.

In your passing, I declare from my full self, and all who surround me, the depth of my sorrow, confusion, anger, and relief.

May your passing honor your liberation.

May your passing honor my liberation.

For the questions that have no answers, the misunderstandings that have no clarification, the difficulties that have no resolution, I call on divine grace.

Beyond hurt and trauma, I remember that the soul is pure. I know your soul has love for me. I allow myself to receive and know your love on soul levels.

I allow any additional healing that wasn't possible in physical form to occur in spirit form.

Whatever lessons we agreed to learn together here, let them be complete.

All is forgiven.

There is peace between us.

Any places where my energy resides in your field are returned to me.

Any places where your energy resides in my field are returned to you. And all is surrounded in light.

All karma between us is clear, immediately and in all lifetimes.

May I reach a place of acceptance and truth in your life and in your death.

May I remember that nature is always changing, as is grief. And this grief can grow into something else—something healing, something beautiful, if I allow it.

Help me know what is mine to heal, and what is ready to be released.

I choose to remember our time together in gratitude.

I will root and bloom wherever I choose to grow, either with the tree that connects us or beyond it. I am divinely protected and blessed wherever and however I choose to grow.

Thank you for all the lessons you taught me about love, truth, loss, boundaries, and power.

Thank you to all of my spirit team and ancestors for giving me the support I need to heal through this experience, to learn and integrate all lessons to the best of my ability, for the highest good of all.

With deepest gratitude, so be it.

Flower essences to complement this prayer:
angelica, borage, Saint John's wort, star-of-Bethlehem,
splendid mariposa lily

PRAYER FOR WHEN YOU FEAR THE APOCALYPSE

This prayer has been helpful to me as I navigate the pain I feel for the state of the world. I find that it supports clarity, a sense of orientation, and hope.

I remember that what is happening here is occurring on both
    levels of form and formless, physical and spirit.

I trust in the regenerative nature of the Earth.

I trust in the infinite wisdom and intelligence of the Earth,
    which exists far beyond the destruction of man.

May the Earth be free of any human-created curses.

I trust the Earth is in the process of taking itself back, and that it
    knows exactly what to do.

I remember that on the spirit level nothing ever dies.

I am learning to hold the paradox of being both a spiritual and physical human being.

Anything can happen, the future is not written, and change is constant.

Beyond linear time and space, there are a plurality of possibilities available to us.

I remember that destruction, even human-created, is part of a natural physical cycle, because humans are nature.

I send love to all the precious elements, plants, and animals. May you be purified, blessed, and surrounded by divine protection.

May the hearts of all humans awaken to exist in love, respect, and care for all sentient beings.

May the collective consciousness shift so that conservation, restoration, and balance can occur immediately.

I pray for the endangered species, and all animals who are leaving; I am so sorry you must leave. I pray for your highest evolution. I thank you for your service here. May you always be remembered and surrounded in light.

I pray for the highest healing of the collective.

I pray for the end of patriarchy and white supremacy.

I pray for oppressed peoples to reclaim their autonomy.

I pray for the equitable redistribution of resources, for the true stewards, caretakers, way showers, and wisdom keepers to come into power.

May we be blessed with strength, courage, vibrant health, and open hearts to fully embrace the possibilities of this time.

May we know that we are here for a reason, that we were made for this time.

Protection to all the children here and coming in.
Protection to all the animals and plants here and coming in.
May all beings be safe, healthy, and free.
Light. Light. Light.

Flower essences to complement this prayer:
gorse, Scotch broom, Alaskan Essences Soul Support

Fire can bring devastation, but it also purifies and readies the Earth for what needs to grow next. Fireweed, *Chamerion angustifolium*, is one of the first plants to regrow after a fire. Fireweed is a nutritive edible plant and its root system stabilizes the soil.

SPELL FOR THE
OPENING INTERLUDE

Moon, moon,
wane and swell,
free to unbind,
empty as a well.

Stillness inside,
tho tornadoes around,
mind is soft,
and body unwound.

I breathe in spaciousness,
feeling peace in the exhale,
fully here and held,
a perfectly balanced scale.

Clean as a whistle,
clear as a bell,
blank as a page,
into the deep deep heart,
    I comfortably dwell.

A crystalline vase,
pristine and clear,
I can pour and fill however
    I like,
boundlessly free of any fear.

All woes brushed bare,
all worries washed away,
I'm open to receive the
    highest,
and ready to play.

Celestial and beloved,
I become my own muse,
free to be starlight,
to co-create whatever
    I choose.

Working with Prayer

IN *THE BLOOM BOOK*, I SHARED THAT HOWEVER YOU are guided to pray and practice is your own unique medicine, and you can trust that this is a natural way to heal. There are many ways to pray; this chapter is intended to spark ideas and inspiration for integrating the *what, why,* and *how of prayer* into praxis. The key is to do it co-creatively—it's between you and the universe—and in ways that feel sacred and empowering. If you already have an existing prayer or spiritual practice, this section should offer further refinement and revelation.

This chapter includes methods for incorporating resonant language—words connected to your heart/higher knowing—as well as methodologies for deep inquiry, healing, and change. We will focus on rituals to accompany your prayers. The subconscious directs the conscious mind and our field to a large extent, and it cannot be accessed through words alone—it must work in concert with the body and the natural world. You get to decide what you are up for with this material. You should expect these practices to bring about change, and if any of this feels like too much for you, simply come back to it later.

One of the reasons I decided to reconsider and reinvest in prayer was because I needed to find a way to consciously engage with the tremendous grief and overwhelm I feel being a human on this planet at this time. I believe these feelings, while uncomfortable, were and are invitations for big shifts. I like to think of them as heart activations. I am not suggesting that prayer is the answer to all the problems in the world, but I am proposing that prayer is a way *to be with all of this*. It is a process that allows us to exist fully embodied here and now, and to be of empowered service if we so choose. Our prayers and healing practices do make a difference. They matter. Even when we may be at our threshold, prayer can be a candle lighting the way forward to new levels of being and also possibility. Our prayers can ignite our commitments, and when we circle together, our collective contribution can be a high offering to ourselves and our world.

PRAYER AS A CO-CREATIVE HEALING PROCESS

Co-creation is the process of consciously creating with life. In this context, co-creation is relational and collaborative. It is not unidirectional or hierarchical. It is reflective of a circular, collective ecosystem, as opposed to a pyramid with humans on top. Unlike egoic manifestation, co-creation utilizes heart, spirit, and soul forces. It is not just about building or adding; it can also include the forces of dissipation and dissolution, as in nature. Nature is constantly creating itself, just as we are in a state of constant becoming. We may assume creation is only happening on the level of physical form, but since we know of the inherent intelligence within nature and space, and because we know that all things are connected and responsive to one another, the full truth is that co-creation is highly dynamic and multidimensional.

Prayer can serve as a catalyst for co-creation. For example:

- **When I make medicine, I'm not just putting plants in water and extracting their healing constituents. I am co-creating with my spirit team, the spirit of the plant(s), the elements, the land, and nature.**

- **When I pray, I am co-creating with the language, feelings, images, and elements of my prayer practice, as well as with the divine.**

- **When I work with a client, we are co-creating together with that person's spirit, their spirit team, and our shared intention.**

- **When a group comes together to pray, we are co-creating not just with the sum of our parts, but exponentially.**

When I co-create, I am not only sending energy out, I am also opening a channel of communication for energy to travel both ways. I inform the field and the field informs me.

Co-creation is concerned with balance, and balance is the optimal state for all life. Where there is harmony, there is natural order, and life can flourish. A tension of opposites is required for creation. Sometimes we experience tension as negative, but it is a necessary and healthy aspect of bringing something into existence. In TCM, it is the opposing forces of the yin and yang that create qi, or energy.

The yin-yang is an ancient symbol that marvelously illustrates the nature of co-creation. The yin-yang is a helix, it is a spiral, it is sexual communion, it is two fundamental opposites of the universe, one of which cannot exist without the other. Yang originally means "the south, sunny side of a mountain," while yin means "the north, shaded side of the mountain." You can't have one side of a mountain without the other. The yin-yang is emblematic of the Ubuntu saying, "I am because you are."

Creation and destruction are the two most potent actions of the universe. And because energy doesn't die, it only transmutes, we can think of destruction and death as vital parts of life, and endings as beginnings.

The relationship between yin and yang is fluid, inviolable, and everlasting. "No insult, threat, accident, or injury can destroy this fundamental rhythm," and we always have the opportunity to connect with this flow.

There was a time when I would wake up every morning with worry in my belly, thinking, "What is going to happen to me today?" If life was a river, I was constantly swimming upstream. I will still occasionally fall into this mindset, but instead now I say, "What do I get to co-create today?" Do you feel the energy of the first statement? To me, it feels sinking, closed, and contracted. How about the energy of the second statement? Notice how the inquiry feels curious, freer, and more open. Life is a river that might not always feel fun or easy, but it's okay for me to let go. I can float downstream with the current, instead of fighting against it.

Co-creation is the progression of thinking to feeling to knowing to being. We get the opportunity to put this into practice whenever we take a moment and reflect on what we are co-creating, through the prayers we speak, see, hear, and live. We can also reflect on this in how we organize our days, show up in the world, and live our lives. These are not insignificant points, for how you do one thing is how you do all things, and small-scale actions set the holographic patterns for the whole system of your life.

We as a culture spend a lot of time thinking about what is wrong and what's not working. It's necessary to take stock of the cracks, but focusing on them keeps us spiraling in an eddy. Co-creation is the next step, moving us forward into what is possible.

What can we see beyond the pain and rupture?

What do we get to co-create that lies outside the range of our trauma?

What are the new constructs we get to co-create that invite balance and peace?

We can honor the hardship, and we can also co-create beyond the bounds of our pain bodies, outside what breaks our hearts and terrifies us. This is not a bypass or means of escapism, but a vehicle for repair and transmutation.

Consumption, Contentment, and Co-Creation

"The ordinary man wants what he does not have."

—THE TAO

Though we may not be aware of it, we are always in co-creation with the Earth—we are always drawing energy from it *and* giving energy back to it. Those of us called to live co-creatively would do well to be aware of the relationship between our prayers and the Earth.

Extractive cycle with the Earth

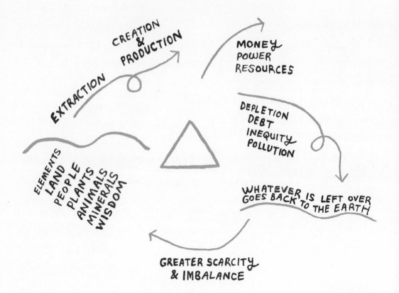

We can also observe how this cycle impacts our attention and focus, especially as they relate to the internet and media. Remember: Energy follows attention, and the social media platforms reinforce comparison culture, envy, and invention of needs. These are scarcity constructs on steroids. They were intentionally created to make us addicted and disempowered, all in the name of engagement.

We've run out of time to be thinking and living like this, asking for more, more, more, without considering the impact or what you are giving back. This mindset is pushing us further out of alignment, bankrupting our spirits and our Earth.

Extractive cycle with our mind

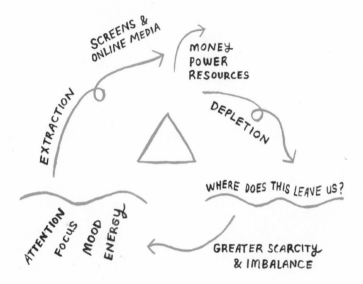

Contentment is a state of happiness and satisfaction. It is knowing you have enough and feeling at peace with your circumstances. Contentment isn't the same thing as complicity. One of the fundamental things I feel people are actually seeking—whether they are conscious of it or not—is to live with peace and a sense of abundance. I think a lot of people *think they want* to be rich, but what they really want is to be free. And you cannot do this unless you have a healthy relationship with contentment.

One main barrier to contentment is our ravenous appetite to consume—not just physical resources, but knowledge and wisdom, information, gossip, relationships (often in the form of "follows"), and even

Co-creative cycle with the Earth

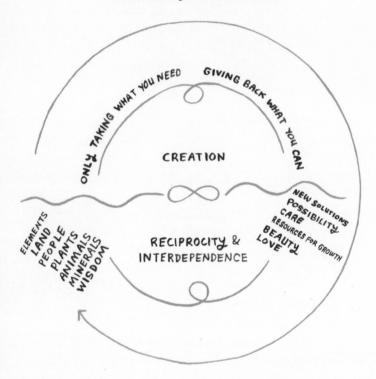

experiences and healing states. *The aspiration behind* our perceived need for power, influence, status, achievement, and, in some cases, healing—this is the major driver of our relationship to consumption.

There is a Native American concept called *wetiko*, which is a Cree term (*windigo* in Ojibway, *wintiko* in Powhatan) that refers to "an evil spirit or person who terrorizes other creatures" in a kind of consumptive cannibalism. It represents a symbolic devouring of life for one's own private purpose or profit. This diabolical madness is behind the horrors of slavery, genocide, and associated acts of mass oppression, and most of the land, plants, animals, elements, and people on our Earth have been shaped by this hunger and greed.

When I speak of consumption in this context, I'm not speaking about survival. Instead, I'm referring to consumption that is superfluous and unchecked in the dominant culture. In the old days, and in some existing traditions today, balance was/is synonymous with survival, and people consumed and stored only what they needed. Prayers functioned as a reflection of their equitable relationship with the Earth. Rituals centered around significant agricultural events such as the fall equinox (September 21 or 22). Being in right relationship with the Earth was essential to the health of the community. A farmer would have prayed for rain to water his field and livestock, but he wouldn't have prayed for more rain than was warranted, or else he risked a flood. Ceremonies were centered around respect for the Earth and maintaining and encouraging balance with all life.

I assume that most people attracted to this book and my work are already aware that money, accomplishment, and status don't buy happiness—in principle, anyway. But these deceptions have severely infiltrated our consciousness, especially in the United States, and the systems reinforcing them are so entrenched (healthcare, politics, education, etc.) that we need to constantly question how we might have fallen into the trap. I know I have to watch myself carefully.

As the West exerted its dominion over the Earth, dangerous precedents for consumption, materialism, and the perpetual need for more were set. Having our basic needs met is one thing, but runaway materialism is another matter. Consuming and making more money do correlate to higher happiness levels, *but only to a point.* **Consumption doesn't equal peace or happiness, it just reinforces the desire for more.**

I frequently see evidence of this insatiable desire for more in the wellness world. (I would know; I am part of it!) I'm sure there are ways in which I've contributed to this culture of constant self-improvement, try as I may to avoid it. Make no mistake: We are overprescribed on self-improvement. This incessant drive toward optimization and self-betterment is presented to us as salvation, but it's really just spiritual ego, materialism, perfectionism, and consumerism in disguise. After a certain point, filtering all life through the lens of your own trauma is myopic and stagnating. It's not in right relationship with the Earth and leads to further imbalance and disease states. If you want to live co-creatively, you have to think bigger picture. Cultivating our prayers from a heart-centered awareness instead of one of ego gratification is a way to avoid this pitfall.

At some point along your path with this practice, I hope you can ask yourself:

What is all that I am seeking really for?

What is it in service to?

Does what I want come at a cost to someone or something else?

Where is the line between self-worship and self-love?

If your contentment is dependent on success, achievement, or status, how do you personally define these terms? What do they mean to you? If you desire influence or power, to what end? Is there liberation or altruism behind these desires, or are they connected to a personal or collective shadow?

To be constantly wanting more, better, bigger, and faster for ourselves can be extractive and depleting, like climbing a never-ending and elusive ladder. Living co-creatively generates reciprocity, balance, and possibility. For example, herbalism has taught me to work with the plants that are growing near me—to trust and work with what's here.

Some questions to tip our awareness into the domain of contentment:

Where might you have what you need?

What is working, going well, that is already in place?

If changes are what you are seeking: Where are they happening? Where do you see and feel the shifts?

Can you focus on and build on these places?

Where are you giving to get? How is that serving you and what/ whom you care about?

If you had "enough," where would you put your time, energy, and resources?

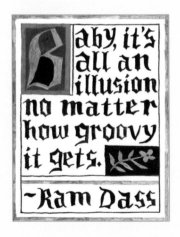

Baby, it's all an illusion no matter how groovy it gets.
~Ram Dass

Living at the level of attachment—which can manifest as a desire for both things and feeling states—is part of being human. The trick is to find ways to balance the extreme pressure to consume with the desire to transcend this level of being as we come into acceptance of our humanness. Thinking in this way opens channels for living in gratitude, which is essential for joy and peace. We will circle back to this in "Gratitude and Joy as a Practice" in a bit.

PRAYER FOR CULTIVATING CONTENTMENT

Dear mother/father god, spirit, and universe,

I call on the powers of my highest self, light, love, truth, nature, and healing.

I call on my angels, guides, ancestors, and all those supporting me.

I believe in a place beyond need and want.

Beyond self-improvement, perfectionism, striving, and success,

a place beyond ladders and pyramids,

on the far side of work altogether.

This is the allow space.

Here is a domain of ISness, of I am THATness.

There's nothing to do and nowhere to go, because you've already arrived.

I welcome myself here;

I let this be a meeting of all that is alive with receptivity inside me.

Impeccably present with all as it should be.

I allow myself the full experience of surrender and letting go.

My whole body exhales;

I release any attachment to: manifestation, more, bigger, better, faster, upgraded, or optimized.

I release the need to know and define in order to feel safe, and
allow all the wisdom that comes from not knowing.

I remember that "ordinary beings want what they don't have."
I cut through the shiny lies capitalism has taught us to believe in
and live for.
I step away from golden carrots, handcuffs, and hamster wheels.
I walk beyond the illusions of instant gratification and
omnipotence.
Past the reaching and grasping, into a place of peace and
contentment.
My whole body relaxes and I am held by the Earth.
The ancestors cheer, for we can commune most easily when we
are at ease.
I trust that I have everything I need.
I know that I have enough because I am enough.
With deepest gratitude, so be it.

The Co-Creative Cycle

As I touched on earlier, nature is, like us, always in a state of co-creation.
There are four stages or seasons of the co-creative cycle: spring, summer, fall, and winter. Creation doesn't equal productivity, and contrary
to popular presumption, co-creation isn't a constant state of doing.
Rather, it's a constancy of being.

Everything has a season. Every season affords us opportunities for
alignment with the energy of that particular time. A cycle of harm can
feel like an interminable season, endless and inescapable. It's easy to

forget we are in seasons of nature, which flow into one another: expanding and contracting, moving in and out, beginning and ending forever.

Working within the co-creative cycle restores our connection to source. I define *source/source energy* as fundamental energy of the undifferentiated self, soul, universe, spirit, heart, god, nature, or divine. It is the vitality flowing through you, connecting you with all life.

A *source connection* is related to the idea of a secure attachment, or heart connection. It is the internal blueprint that maps how source energy, which is the frequency of pure love, runs through you. Each of us has our own unique source connection, which can never be severed, no matter the level of trauma or injury. It is constant, unbreakable, and always available to us. It is only our perceptions and mental limitations that prohibit us from connecting with source energy.

Plants and animals haven't lost their connection to source, but many humans have. The further we evolve away from nature, the greater the chasm from source.

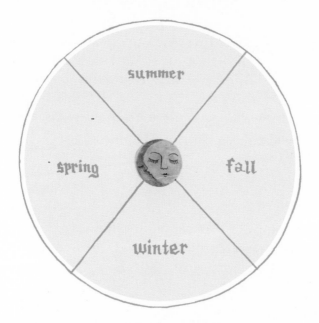

SEASONS OF THE CO-CREATIVE CYCLE

Summer

Element: *fire*

Colors: *red, orange, magenta*

Energetics: *upward-moving, outward-moving, manifesting*

Emotional qualities: *intensity, leonine strength, courage, fullness*

Stage of co-creation: *manifestation, bringing life into form*

Fall

Element: *Earth, metal*

Colors: *gold, Earth hues*

Energetics: *downward-moving, inward-moving, releasing, dispersing*

Emotional qualities: *discernment in holding on versus letting go*

Stage of co-creation: *harvest, enjoying fruits of labor*

Winter

Element: *water*

Colors: *white, silver, black, purple*

Energetics: *grounding, stillness, dormant, void*

Emotional qualities: *restful, dream space, self-care, mystery*

Stage of co-creation: *dormancy, de-manifestation, deep rest, merging with the void*

Spring

Element: *wood*

Colors: *greens, soft yellows*

Energetics: *coalescing, building, conception*

Emotional qualities: *visionary, curiosity, possibility*

Stage of co-creation: *planting seeds, preparing to go outward*

Our culture is tremendously focused on the sunniest season of this cycle—summer. We tend to associate worth, achievement, acquisition, and success with the outward, productive nature of summer. It can be difficult for us to trust the places in the cycle that are abstract, hidden, and mysterious, because these are all domains of the feminine—places we've been taught to ignore, invalidate, and fear. We have been taught that the fiery summer and the harvest of fall are the only seasons of creation that matter. We may even believe that winter equals failure and that rest equals laziness. But there are many opportunities to bring the co-creative cycle into greater balance by embracing all of its stages. For example, in European pagan and folk healing traditions, the crossing points of the seasons—the equinoxes (spring and fall) and solstices (summer and winter), also known as *quarter days*—are considered mystical, liminal realms. These are special windows of time for deep healing work.

I've found loneliness to be one of the scariest emotions for people, and there is a lot of it—increasingly so—in our culture. There is an evolutionary purpose to a fear of isolation. In survival terms, there is safety in numbers and connection. But this sense of separation we feel is exacerbated by our disconnection not just from one another, but from the Earth and nature. When we reorient ourselves within the seasons of the Earth and the co-creative cycle, we strengthen our senses of belonging and connection. We see that we, too, are part of the natural world.

Fully inhabiting the wheel activates co-creative energies and invites a greater source connection, and everything connected to source is successful. Living spherically, growing in all directions, honoring periods of contraction and rest equally with periods of energy and productivity, requires a commitment to living circularly, in communion with nature, not linearly, against it.

Sometimes, to know where we are in the co-creative cycle, we must get very still and quiet. Sometimes we don't get to know where we are in the circle at all: it may feel like we are stuck or in a holding pattern. Here, we must be patient and wait for clarity to orient us.

Seasons of the co-creative cycle inquiries:

What season(s) do you gravitate toward?

What feels safest?

Which one(s) do you avoid? Feel stuck in or overly attached to? How can you invite more balance?

CREATING A SACRED SPACE

Anytime you pray, you open up a sacred channel of communication. Creating a dedicated area or areas for praying can ground your prayer practices and serve as a container for this work to deepen. Sometimes this space is referred to as an *altar*. I was raised to believe that any altar that wasn't Christian was evil, but there is nothing to fear or feel ashamed of in devoting a holy space to co-create as you are guided. You may wish to create individual spaces where you reside, where you work, or near a place you visit in nature. You can also do this when traveling, which is a nice way to connect more deeply with the spiritual dimension of those places you visit, and to co-create with the energies there.

The sacred space I have in my home is situated in front of a window, on the floor. I will light a candle and sit there in the morning. I do the same whenever I pray and make medicine. Sometimes, it's where I write and draw. I am mindful of what energies I bring into this space. I place a cloth over my altar when I go out of town, to protect it (although our two cats do guard it well). The more time I spend in this space, the greater its resonance. I feel it holding me and I trust it.

Tips for creating a sacred space:

- **Choose a quiet spot that has some privacy.**

- **Consider what would help you feel safe and comfortable (e.g., bringing a blanket to wrap yourself in, or a cushion to sit on).**

- Choose a piece of cloth or a small table to lay objects upon.

- Choose some objects that hold significance to you: books, *malas*, stones, shells, or items found in nature, plant medicines, etc.

- Include images of ancestors or any artwork that feels sacred to you.

- Add a candle, incense, dried or fresh flowers, fruit, a bowl of water, or another kind of offering.

My sacred space is where some of my heaviest inner work happens. If I'm immersed in something particularly difficult, either professionally with clients or personally, it's a place to contain the bounds of that work. I can leave that work at the altar. My altar can help me hold what I'm carrying. I don't need to take whatever that work is into the rest of my life. In many ways, my altar offers a way for me to preserve a balance between my work and life.

IDEAS AS SPIRITS

I believe our ideas can be spirits. An idea spirit is like a cosmic baby you bring into the world with its own energy and purpose. It is something you can connect with and nurture, and also let go of when the time comes. You're engaging with the spirit of this book right now. Prayer can serve as a bridge to communicate with our idea spirits and channel them into form.

I have a client, let's call her Alison, who is a talented writer. As we were working together, she was given an assignment to write a book. She decided it would be supportive for me to help her connect with the spirit of her book. To do this, we would go into the field together, invite in her spirit team, and then invite the spirit of her book to join us. It came in through her subtle awareness as a warm feeling in her heart, and a beautiful orange-pink-purple color that would radiate as we listened to it and spoke with it.

In the beginning, the light and feeling of her book were faint, while the voices of fear and self-criticism were louder. But over time, she could differentiate between the fearful voices and the voice of the book more easily. If she felt stuck or uncertain, she could tune in to the spirit of the book for help. If she was on the right path, the light of the book would radiate like a pulsing orb. Eventually, her writing process evolved to include a simple invocation and ritual so that she was centering the spirit of the book as she wrote. And this was her practice as she wrote her final manuscript.

Though it felt unfamiliar at first to trust the process of listening and communicating at this level, it was a place of great growth for my client—to learn to trust a different way of creating that didn't involve force, self-criticism, or self-sacrifice, but receptivity and letting go.

PRAYER TO CONNECT WITH A SPIRIT OF AN IDEA

Dear mother/father god, spirit, and universe,

I call on the powers of my highest self, light, love, truth, nature, and healing.

I call on my angels, guides, ancestors, and all those supporting me.

Dear spirit of _____, I invite you to be part of what I am creating.

Please show me how I can better connect with you and work in service of your spirit.

I am available to receive any insight you'd like to share with me.

Thank you so much for choosing to come through me.

I stand in the vibration of the opportunity to co-create with you.

My energy and attention are attuned to what we are creating. I am clear on what to write and visualize; words and images flow easily from my heart. My mind is clear and sharp. I allow our co-creative process to be easy, fun, and empowering.

All channels to confidence, creativity, ease, grace, prosperity, vision, power, love, truth, help, and healing are open and surrounded in light. I continue to sustain and grow these states within myself, and it feels awesome.

Any blockages are cleared immediately. Any cords connected to harm, slander, misinterpretation, unearned criticism, unworthiness, perfectionism, impostor complex, envy, cruelty, oppression, mental illness, or shadow energies of any kind are closed.

The voices of fear, doubt, comparison, competition, and criticism have no power over me.

I enjoy all the support available to me to offer the highest level of expression and transmission.

May our work be of the highest service to all.

Thank you so much for this opportunity.

With deepest gratitude, so be it.

I've offered up my prayer, now what?

Relax and receive. You have spoken, and the universe has heard you. Even if it feels as though nothing is happening, change is underway. This is the law of observation. In placing your attention on something, an energetic reaction has occurred and the field has shifted.

You may not be noticing anything and it may not be perceptible (yet). It may be a different change than what you were expecting. Look for subtle cues in your field and in your environment.

PRAYER AS A STATE OF GRACE

Prayer may be a place people turn to first, or it may be a last resort. For me, it's both. Sometimes, I am tapped out, overcome, and unable to even articulate the kind of support I need. Other times, I'm not sure what kind of help is called for—whatever it is, it's much bigger than what I know. I come to prayer as a state of grace when things feel too big, over-whelming, or confusing. I come when the loss, grief, or despair feels unbearable, and too much for me to hold. I may be fully collapsing or shutting down. In Buddhism, *suffering is grace*, so these states are related.

There are times when I can barely grasp for a prayer, let alone write one. I may call on the words of someone else. Reading the words of others who are dear to me can be a soothing balm. I simply open a book to a random page, like an oracle. Or I may call a friend and we collaborate on a simple mantra together. I don't put pressure on myself to come up with a solution or force a resolution.

We may feel hopeless, powerless, stuck, or resistant. "This is as far as I can get with this right now." Or "I can't do this alone." We could be working with difficult feeling states like grief, shock, loss, depression, terror, or anger. Prayer as a state of grace can mean keeping the channel open to what you are experiencing, while also creating a safe container so you can work and regulate your way through the moment. Like many trauma survivors, I am prone to obsessing. The more the thought loops spiral, the more out of control I feel. Prayerful repetition can be helpful in these cases.

We can call on divine grace when things are going horribly and we don't know where to turn. When we need a miracle. When we're on our knees, like my friend Alexa as she dealt with her son's cancer treatment, then her own. Miracles don't run counter to the laws of nature—they are very much in alignment with cosmic law. I think miracles, like magic, get a bad reputation because they show just how limited our understanding is of the laws of nature.

Grace is a state that feels divinely ordained. We can access grace, but it holds a special relationship to surrender—to what is beyond ourselves and our control. Grace descends, like an angel wrapping its wings around us, when we are at our most bereft or lost. Encounters with grace remind me that divinity is both intrinsic and extrinsic. Something I've learned about grace on my spiritual path is that, like any state, you can build your capacity for it. The more you lay down your need to control, open yourself up, and surrender, the more grace you can receive and feel. Sometimes there is nothing to be done, nothing to fix. Just bear it. Accept it. This is to let go and let god—and let the grace in.

PRAYER FOR GRACE

Dear mother/father god, spirit, and universe,

I call on the powers of my highest self, light, love, truth, nature, and healing.

I call on my angels, guides, ancestors, and all those supporting me.

May divine grace descend upon me, surround me [or name of loved one], and light my way forward.

Please help me to see, feel, and know all the divine grace, love, and protection that is with me.

It's okay for me to come to this not knowing what I'm doing.

Please show me what I need to get out of this situation.

Please show me what I need to handle this situation.

Please show me how to walk this with courage and integrity.

I am learning how to live through this.

I choose to be extra gentle and caring with myself right now.

All channels to miracles and revelation are open and surrounded in light.

Please give me the bravery, fortitude, and clarity I need to get
through this.

All the resources I need are revealed to me.

My heart remains protected yet open.

I allow this situation to come into balance and resolution naturally.

Please help me to accept the unknowns and uncertainty.

I surrender to what is beyond my knowing and my control.

With deepest gratitude, so be it.

PRAYING WITH THE ELEMENTS

The interdependence of the yin-yang gives rise to the elements. The
elements are the fundamental energies of the universe and the building blocks of all life. The elements play an integral role in many ancient
healing systems and cosmologies, including ancient Egyptian medicine,
which later evolved into the Greek humoral tradition, which influenced
European folk healing and alchemy, homeopathy, flower essence therapy, and Western herbalism.

When praying with the elements, I'm creating a sort of map—a chart
to immerse myself in the frequency of the particular element I want to
commune with. I reference the four elements: earth, air, fire, and water.
In Celtic folklore tradition, there are only three elements: earth, sky,
and sea. In some traditions, there are also the additions of aether, space,
metal, and wood. You may resonate with three, four, or five elements.
Explore what works for you.

The operative word in elemental medicine and healing is *balance*.
We want to encourage harmony between the elements. In our disconnection from nature, we've forgotten our elemental interdependence.

Energetics: *stability, solidity, grounding*

Colors: *green, brown, yellowish-green*

Chakras: *first or root*

Star archetypes: *Taurus, Virgo, Capricorn*

Planets: *Mercury*

Flowers: *corn, madrone, oak*

Scents: *sage, lavender, cinnamon*

Notes: *C*

Animals: *bull, wolf, deer, bear, mouse*

Stones/metals: *agate, petrified wood, emerald*

Natural phenomena: *mountain, cave*

Organs/systems: *digestive*

Times, days, season: *morning, Thursday and Saturday, fall*

Direction: *north*

Energetics: *movement, expansion, dispersive*

Colors: *yellow, white*

Chakras: *fourth/heart and seventh/crown*

Star archetypes: *Gemini, Libra, Aquarius*

Planets: *Saturn*

Flowers: *angelica, pink yarrow, chamomile*

Scents: *cypress, pine, cedar*

Notes: *F, B*

Animals: *hawk, owl, monkey, butterfly*

Stones/metals: *clear quartz, celestite, shungite*

Natural phenomena: *wind, thunder*

Organs/systems: *heart, respiratory*

Times, days, season: *just before sunrise, Wednesday, winter*

Direction: *east*

Energetics: *energizing, stimulating*

Colors: *red, orange*

Chakras: *third/solar plexus and sixth/third eye*

Star archetypes: *Aries, Leo, Sagittarius*

Planets: *the sun, Mars, Jupiter*

Flowers: *sunflower, mullein, calendula*

Scents: *ginger, citrus, frankincense*

Notes: *E, A*

Animals: *lion, tiger, salamander, bee*

Stones/metals: *ruby, carnelian, gold, citrine*

Natural phenomena: *lightning, sunlight*

Organs/systems: *heart, circulatory*

Times, days, season: *midday, Sunday and Tuesday, summer*

Direction: *south*

Energetics: *fluidity, adaptability*

Colors: *blue, silver, black*

Chakras: *second/sacral and fifth/throat*

Star archetypes: *Cancer, Scorpio, Pisces*

Planets: *Venus, Pluto, the moon, Neptune*

Flowers: *aloe vera, lady's mantle*

Scents: *jasmine, lotus*

Notes: *D, G*

Animals: *seal, whale, dolphin, seahorse*

Stones/metals: *moonstone, silver, pearl*

Natural phenomena: *dew, ocean, waterfall*

Organs/systems: *lymphatic, kidneys, skeletal*

Times, days, season: *nighttime, Monday and Friday, spring*

Direction: *west*

When we tend to the elements, and our relationship with them, we come into greater balance within and without. I frequently work with the air element in prayer. You may want to do your own research on how the elements interact within your gestalt.

We know that visualization is vital to creating and sustaining change, internally and in the field. I find tending to all atmospherics (sight, sound, scent, taste) enhances the senses and deepens the prayer experience. Atmospheric considerations are also useful if you are inclined to over-mentalize, like me, or have a hard time tolerating stillness and silence. You certainly don't need to create anything elaborate, or buy a bunch of stuff, to accomplish this. I'm simply offering this chart of elemental correspondences for inspiration.

The symbols on the following page are powerful emblems of elemental integration, and anytime I come across one synchronistically, I regard it as a powerful omen, oracle, or mystery.

Praying with the elements is also useful when supporting an external situation, like a conflict, a place that is in crisis, or a natural disaster. A few summers ago, when California was under siege with fires, my flower essence friend Anna-Maria Pierce sent me a prayer for a group of us to practice together. It was focused on bringing the elements into balance. She kindly gave her permission for me to share it with you.

PRAYER FOR WORKING WITH THE ELEMENTS

We are in the crossing point of our highest power in the point where eternity and infinity meet.

Here we stand in our own divinity; we claim it now and forever.

We embody this reality of the new golden age.

Portals into a new age based on cosmic principles of fairness and life for all that is created by the divine source of life. We envision peace on Earth. Humanity and all kingdoms return to the origin and clarity of consciousness, spirit and soul divine. From this place of empowered love, we declare that we now work with the Directors of the Elementals to restore balance.

FIRE: We urgently ask the Directors of the Fire Elementals to have mercy and please redirect the elements to calmness.

WATER: We urgently ask the Directors of the Water Elementals to come forward to bring relief to the present conditions.

EARTH: We urgently ask the Directors of the Earth Elementals to correspond with the Fire and Water elements to bring balance versus harm and destruction.

WIND: We very urgently ask the Directors of the Wind Elementals to approach balance on the Earth in a gentle way corresponding with the other Directors.

We ask all of humanity to turn their souls, spirit, consciousness, thoughts, feelings, and actions as well as their bodies toward their divine nature. We ask the soul of humanity to entirely release and eliminate distortion and everything that is less than love to turn toward themselves and heal from the wounds, and fear of false and manipulative forces that circle around the globe and beyond.

We stand in union with the divine where the true light streams forth. The light of the creator can flow through one or more portals in our physical and nonphysical bodies. Golden light flowing from the very source into us, directly into the heart, up through the channels and moving through all the systems, gently infusing the wisdom of divine intelligence. We feel this light flowing throughout our body and beyond. Feeling, knowing, seeing it enhancing our higher intelligence.

We, as guardians and stewards of the Earth, for evolutionary progress, present to the Directors of the Elements our
 willingness and determination to work with: souls to souls,
 spirits to spirits, consciousness to consciousness, thoughts
 to thoughts, feelings to feelings, actions to actions, bodies to
 bodies, in alignment.

In love
In divine infinity
Always, for eternity
Growing in harmony and balance, joyfully regenerating
Thanks to the creator, to the multitude of flowers and their
 essences. Thanks to all who work on the divine planes.
Love is the answer
Thank you
Thank you
Thank you

When I map out a prayer, I will pay special attention to my environment afterward. What presents itself—an acorn, a feather, the sound
of water, a reference in a book—can be signs of our prayers being made
manifest. The more we are connected to our subtle awareness and the
natural world, the easier it is to be attuned to the symbols of change
all around us.

River Prayers

I was introduced to Nevada City, California, when I began attending
workshops at the Flower Essence Society, which was founded by Patricia
Kaminski and Richard Katz, who have been stewarding the land there
since 1981. Patricia and Richard are pioneers in flower essence therapy

and hold a deep reverence for the entire ecosystem surrounding their plant medicine work.

The flowers led me to the nearby Yuba River and I fell in love. This is the ancestral homeland of the Nisenan tribe, on the Nevada City Rancheria, some of the first guardians of the waters, before the Spanish arrived in the late eighteenth century, and before more white people came to mine for gold. Gold is the ore of purity and presence. The Yuba once contained more gold than any stream in the United States. By the late 1800s, it was stripped clean.

But the Yuba still holds great power. The giant, sun-bleached granite rocks of the river were carved by glacial tides, giving them a softness. Lying in them makes you feel as if you are being held by the landscape. The water, icy and pristine, descends from the snowmelt higher up, and ranges in color from arctic blue to aquamarine to emerald green. The Sierra Nevada region is home to spectacular flora and fauna. The rocky path to the river is lined with California poppy, manzanita, and wild rose. Blackberries grow juicy and plump. You may spot a red-tailed hawk soaring above, or a tenacious western gray squirrel looking for a snack. The air is thin and dry. When the sun hits the leaves, the forest is atomized with scents of bay laurel, juniper, and ponderosa pine. There is a wildness to this place that sharpens my awareness and makes me feel open and unbridled like nowhere else.

A few years ago, I decided to create a special prayer ceremony at the river. I wrote to my community and asked them if they'd like to be involved. I told them they could give me a prayer, which I would bring to the river, and offer up. Theirs would be said along with my own prayer for the river. Here is what I offered.

PRAYER FOR THE YUBA

Dear mother/father god, spirit, and universe,

I call on the powers of my highest self, light, love, truth, nature, and healing.

I call on my angels, guides, ancestors, and all those supporting me.

May you always flow with abundance.

May you always run wild and pure.

May you always be protected.

May you remain a safe sanctuary for all the plants, animals, and people who dwell within and around you.

May you be free of any human-created curses.

Light to all human beings who are touched by your waters near and far.

Light from all beings who support you; we offer our highest blessings.

May the quickening of collective awakening continue, to open the eyes and hearts of humans, to bring us back into balance with this land, water, and all its inhabitants.

Gratitude for the original ancestors who cared for you, Nisenan peoples.

Gratitude for the intersection of all elements: Earth, Air, Fire, and Water, here. May this river remain a perfect balance between the elements. May this balance radiate outward immediately and infinitely.

May you continue to help all life come into cosmic balance.

With deepest gratitude, so be it.

I was filled with great peace after the ceremony and sat with the rocks for some time. Though I wasn't expecting it, the channel of communication remained open. Would you like to hear what the river said back to me?

These are the times of traveling light and treading even lighter. The karmic weight of everything has been magnified, for better or for worse. Rapid change is upon us. Be prepared for it sooner than you expect. Don't expect things to get easier, but know the difference between coursing up versus downstream. Don't be afraid. Everyone is given everything they need to fulfill their work in each lifetime. There are many with assignments far heavier than yours, so do your best to be of service to all beings. Don't assume anything. There are infinite realities beyond your knowing. Therefore, you must have compassion in all matters.

If you keep your heart open to the peril of the Earth and her inhabitants, your heart will break again and again, but the cost of this is far better than if you keep your heart shut off from reality. Many beings are leaving this plane, which on the material level looks like horrific destruction, but this is also a natural cycle. On another level, a balancing is occurring, a purification, and nothing in the spirit world ever dies.

We know it's not an easy time to be here and we understand you want to leave sometimes. You are needed here, though. You have work to do. More will be revealed later as you are able to receive it.

Physical offerings in honor of this ceremony were made to Nevada City Rancheria and the South Yuba River Citizens League.

My time spent in Nevada City and the Yuba has taught me many things, including how to be in greater reciprocity with the Earth. Now, wherever I explore, I consider how I can give back to the ecosystem that has given something to me. Imagine what we could co-create if we traveled in reciprocity. What if this became a prescribed norm, like a gratuity, in which everyone participated? That's a micro contribution that could lead to a macro change. Wherever you root and roam on this Earth, please know that these places need our love and protection immediately.

Some questions to consider for being in reciprocity with the Earth, wherever you travel:

Who was here before you? What is their history?

What plants and animals live here?

Where is the money you are spending here going?

Are there any people or organizations doing work that matters to you? Rewilding, promoting indigenous culture, preserving the ecosystem, etc.?

What are the opportunities for reciprocity here?

Hugging the Yuba, Nevada City, California

PRAYER AND PLANT MEDICINE

Prayer and plant medicine are inseparable to me. One doesn't exist without the other. When I first started working with flower essences, I was guided to sit with them in prayer. Unlike modern medicinal solutions, these remedies encouraged healing by being present with them. I soon learned that the more time I spent with a plant, the more the nature of its unique medicine was revealed to me. Prayer plays a role in all facets of working with plant medicine: medicine making, formulation, selection, and application. In prayer, I am in the liminal, receptive place with the plants to accept and transmit love and wisdom.

There are many applications of plant medicine, which can be in the form of:

Tinctures—made by extracting physical constituents of the plant into alcohol, apple cider vinegar, or glycerin

Teas—steeped infusion from plant matter and water

Powders

Resins and burnables (e.g., incense)

Oxymels—equal parts honey and apple cider vinegar (hawthorn and rose hip are popular herbs for this)

Foods as medicine

Mists and hydrosols

Oils—plants infused with a carrier oil such as almond, jojoba, or apricot kernel

Essential oils—potent extractions of plants (please use mindfully as EOs require much plant matter to create)

Salves—plants infused with oil, along with beeswax

Poultices and liniments

Baths and soaks

Plant spirit medicines—as with flower essences or attunement with a plant

> **"Each tree, shrub, and herb, down**
> **even to the grasses and mosses,**
> **agreed to furnish a remedy for one of the diseases named,**
> **and each plant said:**
> **I shall appear to help Woman when she**
> **calls upon me in her need."**
>
> —CHEROKEE PROVERB

Intentions

My formal education in plant medicine started with an apprenticeship with my flower essence and herbalist teacher, Claudia Keel, in 2013. Fresh out of graduate school, I was keen to get my hands in the Earth, literally, and integrate my mental health counseling training with plants. I knew that flower essences would serve as the bridge between my spiritual and Western training, connecting what I knew with my mind with what I felt in my heart. Jane had introduced the idea of setting intentions within the therapeutic landscape to me years before, but it was my work with the flowers that taught me the role intentions play in working with plant medicine.

Intentions are the purpose of what you are doing or creating. Intention is the energy *behind* what you co-create. It is the core issue or situation you want to address. Intention informs the vibrational signature of your medicine, prayer, or offering. Intentions are the seeds we plant. These seeds go into the Earth, and are transmitted and transmuted elementally.

I try to keep my intentions simple and elegant. We must be both clear in intention and detached from the outcome. Letting go of a desired outcome frees up more energy for our prayers to work their own magic. In clarifying your intention, consider using affirmative statements, because we are working with resonance, and in the flow of energy we would like to attract. For example, "I am open to seeing how I can best support myself in this situation." Sometimes, I will ask for the best thing for me/someone else to come to me. We want everything we offer up to be for the highest good and healing.

In many ways, the intention behind your work and prayer is more important than the words themselves. Not all is as it seems in our world, and seeing what's true and real requires us to be able to tell when something is incoherent. We must look to see when there is an incongruence between the intention, or the energy behind something, and what is being presented. That is why so much of this book is dedicated to helping you align with words that are embodied and connected to your heart.

Remember the observer effect. Focusing on anything causes it to change at the subconscious/subatomic level. Intentional words → co-creation → alchemy → change in the field.

Flower Essences for Prayer

Flower essences are like liquid meditations or prayers. They are great shifters of consciousness, and may invite healing through adjusting our perspective and broadening our awareness. When making medicine, the elements that are part of the process become part of the healing signature of the essence. So, the prayer and words I bring into my flower essence–making inform the energetics of it, and become part of the medicine itself. Likewise, I am in that imaginal realm when making medicine, and am listening, open to receive any information that wants to come through. Like prayer, medicine making is reflexive, not one-way. And like prayer, it is the relationship we cultivate with the plants that matters most.

I observe the continued proliferation of vibrational medicine in our culture and see flower essences as a medicine of the future. They are energetic, highly sustainable, accessible, safe, and potent.

Making and taking flower essences is a wondrous exercise in being in receptivity and reciprocity with the plant kingdom and Earth. This is a perfect time to practice deep listening—a form of prayer in and of itself. What is the flower saying or showing to you? What about the land, or the way the wind is blowing? How does the sun feel? If you open to the forces of nature, you will discover that they have already initiated a relationship with us. All you need to do is open up and receive it.

Again, *energetic* refers to the subtle, vibrational, emotional, or bio-electric charge of something. The energetics I consider supportive to a rich prayer practice are: openness, presence, grounding, relaxation, connection to heart/source/nature, and connection to our guides.

Flower Essences That Support Prayer

Delta Gardens celandine—*Enhances many aspects of communica-tion; for self-expression; receiving inspiration or higher thought; for communication blocks and misunderstandings.*

Bach cerato—*"The 'intuition flower' takes us from indecisiveness to inner certainty. [Develops] the Soul's potential for inner certainty, trust in the inner voice and intuition."* (M. Scheffer, **The Encyclopedia of Bach Flower Therapy**)

Alaskan Essences comandra—*Indications: visionary abilities unde-veloped or ungrounded and therefore of no practical use; focus of one's perceptions limited to the gross, material aspects of the physical world. Healing qualities: support for maintaining the necessary perspective on both the seen and unseen worlds as we move through the current dimensional shift opens the heart to be a bridge between the third and fourth dimensions; helps us develop our potential to see the physical world from a higher perspective.*

Flower Essence Society forget-me-not—*Positive qualities: awareness of karmic connections in one's personal relationships and with those in the spiritual world; deep mindfulness of subtle realms; soul-based relation-ships. Patterns of imbalance: lack of connection with souls in the spiritual world; loneliness and isolation due to death of a loved one; soul myopia.*

Delta Gardens moonlight currant, "Heart Link #5"—*Awakens emerging heart to higher functioning; "seeing" with the heart develops; energy made available for cleansing of heart blockages and wounds.*

Bach rock water—*"'The Flexibility Flower,' from dogmatic discipline to attentiveness. [Develops] the Soul's potential for flexibility and inner free-dom."* (M. Scheffer, The Encyclopedia of Bach Flower Therapy)

Flower Essence Society star tulip—*Positive qualities: sensitive and receptive attunement; serene soul disposition, inner listening to others and to higher worlds, especially in dreams and meditation. Patterns of imbalance: inability to cultivate quiet inner presence, lack of attune-ment or soul insight, unable to meditate or pray.*

Sometimes, we are called to prayer when we are experiencing feeling states outside of our window of resilience. This is a state of crisis, in which we are past the threshold of being able to emotionally regulate and cope. I've found flower essences to be trusted and effective allies for acute trauma responses. For these times, I may reach for the following formulas: Bach Rescue Remedy, FES Post-Trauma Stabilizer, Alaskan Essences Soul Support, Alexis Smart Safe and Sound, Delta Gardens Emergency Protection, and Perelandra ETS Emergency Solution for Humans (they also have a formula for animals). I always keep a few of these on hand in my herbal first-aid kit.

Plant and Prayer Rituals: Breathwork, Herbal Bath, and Dreamwork

A ritual is any practice you perform with intention. Prayer is the planting of our seeds and ritual is how we help them grow. Rituals connect the physical world with the nonphysical one. To me, rituals serve as a way to strengthen my relationship to my heart/source/spirit. Rituals serve many functions. They nurture creativity, enhance presence and deep-listening skills, and help us process challenging emotions or situations. They assist us in cultivating reciprocal relationships with the Earth, dismantling external power structures and restoring inner wisdom and guidance. Rituals can also serve as ways to honor and strengthen our connection to the spirit world, our ancestors, and nature.

We used to think that memories were static, but we now know that when we bring memories into our awareness, we modify them. If we access a troubling experience and pair it with a different intention, along with a supportive sensory experience as in with ritual, we're reprocessing the troubling memory with more neutral and positive cues, and the negative association can be discharged. This is known as memory reconsolidation.

Here are three plant rituals where prayer can play a role. They can be performed at times that feel potent to you, or anytime you need more support.

BREATHWORK AND FLOWER ESSENCE EXERCISE

I've found creating resonant language and using it in tandem with breathwork and flower essences to be particularly useful in helping us relax and regulate. Breathwork can help us ground, be present, and, if necessary, complete a stress cycle, as opposed to staying in fight, flight, freeze, or fawn.

This exercise will engage the first chakra, our center for feeling safe and secure. The intention of this exercise is to build your capacity to experience greater safety, presence, and connection to the Earth.

Choose a flower essence that you feel called to, and take 3 drops.

You can create your own short mantra to accompany this exercise, or use: "I am here. I am clear. I am held by the Earth."

Set yourself up to sit or lie comfortably and quietly for about five minutes. Set a timer if that's helpful.

Lower your gaze or close your eyes.

Call in your spirit team and the spirit of the plant(s) with which you are working.

Visualize a tube of light running from the top of your head (crown chakra) all the way through the central line of your body to your perineum (root chakra) and emanating down into the Earth. This is your pranic tube.

Begin by taking a long, slow inhale and exhale, letting your chest and belly soften and expand. Utilize a box breathing pattern: inhale for four counts, hold for four counts, exhale for four counts, hold for four counts. Keep breathing as you envision the light running through your core channel. You may visualize it running in both directions.

After a few rounds of the box breathing, begin adding in the mantra.

Inhale: "I am here." Holding the breath: "I am clear." Exhale: "I am held by the Earth." Holding the breath: silence. Repeat this five to seven times, or for three to five minutes.

End by taking a big inhale and exhale.

When finished, allow your root chakra to go back to a comfortable neutral position. Thank your spirit team and plant spirit. Spend a few minutes reflecting or journaling on any sensations or insights that arose for you.

FLOWER ESSENCE BATH RITUAL

This ritual can be adapted to a foot bath if you don't have a bathtub.

Bathing culture was very popular throughout the ancient world, and extensive bathing practices like exfoliating, moisturizing, applying clays and oils, and taking steam, were considered essential for good health. (Perhaps this is the origin of the belief that cleanliness is closer to godliness?) You may assume that baths don't have much medicinal merit, but they are an incredibly potent method of not only delivering medicine into your body—your skin, or integumentary system, is the body's largest organ system—but also promoting nervous system downregulation. (Read: deep levels of rest, relaxation, and healing.) Further, one is most responsive to subtle medicine (or any medicine) while in a relaxed, parasympathetic state. According to flower essence pioneer Gurudas, bathing in flower essences is equivalent to taking a larger dose of a remedy, because the bathing dilutes the essence (which makes it travel more deeply), energizes it, and spreads it over the entire surface of the body.

Water stores and transmits energy, and it holds intention especially well. Our ancestral liquid matrix is seawater, and adding sea and/or Epsom salts to your bath creates an environment rich in negative ions that reduces pain and fatigue, detoxifies, eases muscle tension, and lowers cortisol. Energetically, salt has purifying and drawing-out properties, making it a good choice for balancing anything that might be stuck or building up in your system.

As your bath is filling with warm water, add 1–2 cups of Epsom salt and/or 1/2 cup of sea salt.

Select a flower essence you are working with or feeling drawn to and set it aside.

Sit quietly and reflect on any prayers or mantras you may have been working with today, or allow some prayerful language to arise. You're going to *charge*, or infuse, the water with these words. Maybe you are learning how to feel safe inside your body and build your capacity for feeling peaceful. You could create something simple such as, "I give myself permission to fully let go and be held by the water, this medicine, and myself. I allow myself to feel safe and peaceful." Check in with yourself about the language: Does it feel resonant? When it feels right, take a few deep breaths, and place 7 drops of the flower essence into the water. Place just your hands in the water and recite your prayer three times.

Get into the bath, trying to keep the mind soft. You may return to your breath and your prayer as you need to. Soak for at least fifteen minutes.

As the water is draining, visualize any old energy, blockages, and fears that are no longer serving you being pulled out of your body and going down the drain. Feel the magnetic pull of the water and gravity taking anything that was prohibiting safety and peace back to the Earth for the Earth to recycle. Thank the water, salt, and flower essence for helping you.

As you towel off, notice how you feel. Do you feel softer, quieter, calmer? Where and how?

DREAMWORK RITUAL

A lot of healing work happens while we are sleeping. Our glymphatic system, the lymphatic system of our central nervous system, is constantly filtering toxins from the brain. During sleep, though, our norepinephrine levels decline, leading to "an expansion of the brain's extracellular space," which literally creates more fluidity within the brain and entire central nervous system. Our subconscious does deep work for us as we sleep, helping us work out things we may not be able to deal with in our waking lives. Our subconscious mind is always "on" and is especially active during sleep, when it joins forces with our astral body in dreaming. Fellow herbalist Vanessa Chakour shared with me that sometimes, before bed, when she wants to work something out in her dreams, she will ask, "What do I need to see to heal?" The ritual that follows is inspired by this simple inquiry.

Before bed, consider an issue or inquiry you would like to explore and call in your spirit team.

Place paper or a journal and a pen nearby.

Create 1–3 lines of prayer language such as, "I welcome into my dreamtime any symbols or memories that help me remember my confidence and power. Please show me what I need to heal my relationship with feeling unsure of myself."

You may want to work with a flower essence such as mugwort or star tulip. Take 3 drops as you fall asleep.

Upon waking, be still and try to recall as much of your dreams as possible. You can take a few drops of the flower essence for extra assistance. Jot down some notes.

This ritual can be repeated a few nights in a row with the same language if necessary.

Alternative Prayer Rituals

Maybe sitting in silence for an extended period of time is not your thing—no problem. Here are some other prayerful ritual ideas. You can pair prayer with:

- Walking—See if you can remain quiet, present, and in rhythm with your breath. This is also a good time to listen to recorded prayers.
- Dancing—Express your prayer through movement.
- Painting, drawing, or any media
- Gardening or working with plants
- Journaling—Writing can be a natural vehicle for imprinting your will into co-creation.
- Watching the flame of a candle or fire
- Listening to ambient or soft classical music

RESOURCED FOR RESILIENCE

Our resources give us our capacity for living. They encompass all the ways we've positively adapted to our environment to survive and thrive. Our resource level is the sum total of those proficiencies we have inherited and/or earned. Being well resourced means to be securely equipped to meet the demands of life and one's circumstances. There are different kinds of resourcing: internal and external; inherited and earned; emotional, energetic, physical, financial, and social. For example, I work with a lot of folks who are either waking up to an abusive relationship, are in the process of leaving one, or are dramatically lowering contact with or cutting off an abusive person/system. Making these bold moves in the name of one's healing requires resources. (And it's ableist to assume that anyone can just leave an abusive relationship. You have to be resourced—usually significantly—to do so.)

When I work with clients, I always assess their resource level and try to get a sense of those factors that are protective versus prohibitive in their healing. Do they have a supportive family or community, or do they feel isolated? Do they have good somatic awareness of themselves, or do they feel disconnected from their bodies? Are they in a place of financial security, or one of hardship? These are some of the areas I consider in my holistic overview. A goal in my work is to help people identify and also build their level of resourcing, with an emphasis on internal resourcing.

It's common to be overly identified with the areas in which we are under-resourced, but I find that exploring where we are fortified is quite valuable. Everyone has different strengths and weaknesses, and it's important to remember that there is resourcing that is within our control and resourcing that is more externally influenced by systems and norms we cannot control. All the ways you heal and come into balance build your resources, and prayer can be a worthwhile way to develop new and stronger tools.

Becoming better resourced is a way of adapting to our circumstances and challenges. Like plants with their own unique vibrational signature, we also stretch, spread, and strengthen. We learn how to respond in order to survive. The better your resources, the bigger the evolutionary reward, and one of these rewards is resilience.

To live and to love well requires resilience. If walking through the world with an open heart is important to you, you will need a good amount of resilience to manage it. Prayer is a rich training ground for strengthening our connection to our intuition, higher awareness, and hearts. Resilience is a natural result of this connection. It is an outcome of the higher communion with self/heart/spirit and of living co-creatively.

Resilience is an elevated response to stress or conflict. It sustains our energy and builds us up. The natural world demonstrates resilience for us. Nature is resilient because it is eternal. It knows how to renew and regenerate. It works in accord with creation and destruction. Nothing in nature is wasted; everything plays a role. Beyond the binary of good or bad, everything has a purpose. We, too, can learn to stay open to and hold all the parts of ourselves as whole, undifferentiated selves.

Trauma can harden us, stiffening our most subtle structures and fooling us into thinking we need to constantly brace ourselves for what's coming next. Hardness doesn't lend itself well to weathering this time and place, or thriving here. But I do witness the collective softening, opening, and reconstructing. As we learn to integrate more shadow, we awaken to our resilience. During moments of collapse, we find a way to make empowered choices: of curiosity over criticism, of compassion instead of flagellation, of miracles in spite of misery. We can make the choice to adapt rather than regress.

Plantain, *Plantago major*, grows close to the ground, and though plants don't deserve to be mistreated, plantain thrives by being disturbed and stepped on. Medicinally, it is used to ease coughs and heal wounds and skin irritation.

Here, I will quote our divine mother curandera Dr. Clarissa Pinkola Estés, who reminds us, encouragingly, that there have never been more awakened souls than there are right now across the world, and we "are fully provisioned and able to signal one another as never before in the history of humankind."

One of the gifts of our time is the ever-expanding range of emotions and states we humans get to experience, name, express, and integrate. Colors are vibrational frequencies, just like emotional states. I see and feel emotions as colors—in myself, other people, plants, and animals. Some emotions are sunny and bright, others are murky and shadowy. Some emotions oscillate between colors. No color is unwelcome—all make up the divine rainbow of the collective emotional and energetic

THE UNCOMMON BOOK OF PRAYER

experience. In nature, a rainbow manifests from just the right balance of elements, and a particular ratio of both light and darkness is necessary in order to perceive its full spectrum.

If every emotion has a unique color on the spectrum, I welcome the rainbows within and without. When we allow ourselves to be with whatever is arising within us, we create space for great vibrancy and adaptability.

One major state that stands in opposition to resilience is perfectionism. Perfectionism isn't a friend to resilience. If resilience is malleable and self-healing, the energetics of perfectionism are like opaque glass—fragile and obscured. My perfectionism looks and feels like an icicle—a hardened, frozen cloud. As a self-identified perfectionist in recovery, it's been a long road to letting go of being perfect, of healing and doing life perfectly.

This is a lesson many of us are learning. For the women-identified, many of us were groomed to be "good girls," docile and dependent, thin and beautiful, like infantile living dolls. For those of us who can, we must leave behind whatever tethers us to the spell of the fawn. We must fully inhabit our own bodies and lives as individuated, empowered adults. We must relearn how to feel safe in ourselves: to mess up and also forgive ourselves. We can be both fully human and accountable. Here, I think of oak flower essence. Oak is an incredibly durable wood, but its strength overrides flexibility. Its rigid branches are more likely to break during a storm than those of other trees. Oak teaches us to know when to bend and when to hold strong in tough times.

I meet a lot of gentle souls who have survived so much, and they would refuse to mistreat anyone the way they were mistreated. But, instead, they internalize the cycle of harm. You get to decide if forgiving those who've hurt you is in your best interest, but regardless, I do

feel it's a healthy and liberating act to forgive yourself. But for many of us, self-forgiveness is elusive. Personally, I found that in order to access true resilience, I had to learn to forgive myself. Perhaps you can relate, and you too have the opportunity to forgive yourself for not doing life perfectly. Maybe you also spin stories that have tricked you into believing that if you'd done it perfectly in the past, you'd be better off now. (Flower essences to assist with guilt and self-forgiveness are Bach pine and willow, respectively.)

No one is doing life perfectly or has all the answers for how to live and heal through this time—as alluring as the sparkly images and stories on social media may be. Not everything is a referendum on my ability to be perfect. The waves will keep coming. I've come to expect and welcome them. Disappointment does not equal deficiency. Not getting what you want does not equal punishment.

Emotional states that are friends of resilience are: compassion, care, love, ease, comfort, curiosity, trust, humor, and especially self-forgiveness.

What are my resources?

Where am I in resistance to life? To myself?

Where may I be withholding forgiveness from myself?

What do I need to support my own resilience?

How is my resilience connected to the resilience of my community? The Earth?

How do we access, sustain, and build resilience collectively?

GRATITUDE AND JOY AS A PRACTICE

Building our capacity for gratitude and joy aids in resilience. It offers us the ability to draw from our reserves when we may be running on empty. Cultivating gratitude and joy equips you with more resources for the times when life inevitably doesn't go your way. Choice is a gateway to change, and gratitude is a choice we can make that shifts us from victim to empowered consciousness, and from lower vibratory states to higher ones like joy.

I see gratitude as a precursor to joy for several reasons. There are many factors (genetic, social, economic, environmental, etc.) that are beyond our control that can impede our joy. But research shows that a consistent gratitude practice can actually help us shift our perspective, despite our conditions and conditioning, and improve our sense of optimism and well-being. Gratitude can reduce rumination about past trauma. And it has been shown that prayer can increase levels of gratitude.

As a healing practitioner, many people come to me wanting to "feel better." To do so, first we need to investigate what "feeling better" is really about—a clearer articulation offers more direction than a vague description. Second, we need to consider our expectations around "feeling better," as it may not: a) be a magical world we wake up to one morning and b) be a realistic goal to feel all the time. Life is not an ever-ascending straight line, but a roller coaster of waves and circles.

What does feel realistic to me is to cultivate the ability to recognize when things do feel better—as we identify moments that feel more hopeful, comfortable, and easy. Can you take a moment to be grateful here and now? To let yourself savor the warm heat of the sun on your skin, to receive a hug from a friend, or to experience pride from a small victory at work? The more embodied and present we are with ourselves, the easier it is to feel gratitude for the small things that can fill our proverbial glasses. Over time, cultivating your capacity for gratitude and joy adjusts your resting being baseline. With commitment, you can create a new default position.

It can be challenging to access gratitude when we are experiencing strong lower vibratory states and extreme stress, and there will be times where being in gratitude and joy is inaccessible, or not in alignment with what's happening in your life. If you do feel that you're in the window of opportunity for this practice, know that it might require a "fake it until you make it" approach. A simple way to integrate gratitude into your life is by adopting a gratitude practice. This means taking a few moments to reflect on what you're grateful for—think of it as its own type of prayer. It may sound super basic, but this method can work serious miracles. Here are some gratitude practice tips:

- Write down what you're grateful for or say it out loud. This enhances the mind's and the body's recognition of what you are stating.

- Start off small. It's okay if you need to be grateful for a cup of coffee or a snuggle with your cat.

- If you need inspiration, consider: people, exchanges, places, animals, plants, weather, your home, or your community.

- If you're reflecting on something that felt hard or didn't go your way, is there any place in that experience where you can find some gratitude? This can mean feeling proud of how you showed up in the face of a challenge or finding something about the experience that gave you more clarity.

- Consistency is key, so find a time of day that works best for you and see if you can commit to a daily practice.

- Consider doing this practice and reflecting on the previous week, summarizing the week in gratitude.

- Consider doing this practice and reflecting on the week ahead, looking to the future with gratitude.

- Challenge yourself. When you feel resistant, see if you can choose this practice over resentment, hopelessness, despair, etc.

Honoring the Collective Emotional Rainbow and Balancing Polarity

Balancing polarity is a way of holding paradox—of being in "both/and" thinking, as opposed to binary "either/or" thinking. Centering gratitude and joy as a practice is not about reinforcing positivity to the point that we negate dark or negative feelings. Emotions like rage and grief can be sacred. Joy can be medicine. Both of these things can be true simultaneously. Both, along with all feeling states, are part of the human experience, and all emotions are part of the collective emotional rainbow. In the Yoruba tradition, the goddess Oya lives inside the rainbow. She is associated with destruction as well as transformation.

"We need pleasure to heal trauma."

—KIMBERLY ANN JOHNSON, AUTHOR OF *CALL OF THE WILD: HOW WE HEAL TRAUMA, AWAKEN OUR OWN POWER, AND USE IT FOR GOOD*

How do we feel good given the current circumstances? I, myself, am figuring out how to hold a field of balance with more space for joy amid the morass we are in.

Places I remain in inquiry:

Is there a limit to how good we can feel given the state of things?

How well can one truly be within a sick society?

What do I do with guilt I experience sometimes about feeling joy and higher vibratory states?

How do we find joy in the act of overcoming oppression?

How do we bear witness to what is happening and also feel joy?

I don't have answers to these questions, but I do know that those of us doing the work of waking up must learn to hold an increasingly strong and significant container for pain *and* pleasure, for shadow as well as light. We want to grow our capacity for both in a balanced way, knowing all along that we can't have one without the other.

It is necessary to have relationships with the shadow and our trauma, but we don't need to be overly oriented around them. We must continually find ways to sustain and build higher vibratory states within ourselves and our communities. While it's healthy to challenge yourself, you can't shame, guilt, punish, or hate yourself into feeling good. It doesn't work like that. In homeopathy, "like heals like." Pure states of pleasure and joy don't arise from self-abnegation or self-sacrifice.

Yes, it's important not to bypass certain emotions—we can't skip grief, for instance, when we lose a loved one. We will have to let ourselves fully feel that. But we can also make a choice to move through grief, when it's appropriate, and to feel more joy.

One way to work with challenging or lower vibratory states is to look at them in terms of the polarity they occupy within ourselves, and to work toward neutralizing or balancing them. Sometimes, it can be difficult to name what we are feeling, and what states we would like to center and feel instead. For simplicity's sake, I have divided these into lower and higher vibratory states. Lower in this context doesn't equal bad, as each state has a purpose.

What words jump out at you?

Where do you feel attached?

Where do you feel you could come into greater balance?

LOWER VIBRATORY STATES	HIGHER VIBRATORY STATES
Anger	Acceptance
Anhedonia	Accountability
Anxiety	Balance
Apathy	Comfort
Bitterness	Compassion
Confusion	Confidence
Denial	Connection
Depression	Contentment
Despair	Courage
Distrust	Creativity
Doubt	Curiosity
Energetic depletion	Detachment
Fatigue	Ease
Fear	Empowerment
Grandiosity	Energy
Grief	Excitement
Guilt	Expansion
Hatred	Feeling free
Jealousy	Flow
Lack of clarity	Forgiveness
Negativity	Fun
Obsession/overattachment	Grace
Powerlessness	Gratitude
Rejection	Hope
Resistance	Joy
Self-pity	Laughter
Shame	Letting go
Stuckness	Love

LOWER VIBRATORY STATES (continued)	**HIGHER VIBRATORY STATES** (continued)
Unhealthy pride	Magic
Unworthiness	Mystery
Vengeance	Neutrality
Weakness	Openness
Worry	Optimism
	Passion
	Play
	Pleasure
	Pride
	Spaciousness
	Strength
	Surrender
	Wonder

A Pre-Prayer Process:
Balancing Polarity

This is an exercise inspired by my teacher Jane's teacher, Leslie Temple-Thurston, who worked extensively with polarity and ascended frequency states.

Complex trauma survivors tend to default to the negative. We have to work harder to raise our resting baseline to a higher level, and we may need to consistently remind ourselves of what we are co-creating in the present moment. Even if we are feeling bad, that is an opportunity *to choose how to respond* to how we are feeling, rather than to simply react. One way to encourage this is to see where we are being drawn into the negative, name it, and find the language that feels like a natural counterbalance to that state. From here, we can arrive at a place of balance.

For instance, let's say you are struggling with feeling crummy.

Step one) *Allow the specific words to emerge that name how you feel: despairing, frustrated, and doubtful.*

Step two) *See if it feels okay to get a little closer to these feelings. Notice where they are presenting in your body. Maybe you notice an uneasiness in your belly and a heaviness on your chest. Is there any imagery that goes with these sensations?*

Step three) *Allow the words to emerge that feel like a counterbalance to despairing, frustrated, and doubtful. Is it joy? Is that not quite right? How about hope—yes, that resonates. What is the counterbalance to frustrated? Is it ease? Yes, good. And doubt? That's trust and confidence. Now you have: hope, ease, trust, and confidence.*

Step four) *Now we're going to create a short mantra—remember, a mantra is like an abbreviated prayer—with these four words. This would be a good place to include the affirmative language from Chapter III. Be sure to keep checking in with yourself to determine if the words you chose feel like the right fit.*

> *I'm open to being shown how to feel hopeful.*
> *I allow myself to feel and experience ease with my workday.*
> *I am learning how to trust myself and feel confident.*

Step five) *Here is your polarity-balancing language. You can refer back to it as it feels relevant. Maybe you write it on a Post-it note where you can see it or jot it down in your journal.*

Sometimes it's not possible to override your biology with language, and you can't think your way out of emotional dysregulation. This exercise may need to be paired with something somatic, like breathing, tapping, going for a walk, or doing some kind of mindful movement.

Questions to help you arrive at the resonant language for your prayer:

What does joy [or other higher vibratory state] look like to you?

How does it feel in your body?

What does it look like in your world?

How does it manifest in your relationships?

When, where, why, and how do you feel joy?

What are your negative stories, beliefs, or blockages to experiencing joy?

What do you feel you need to experience joy?

PRAYER FOR CENTERING GRATITUDE AND JOY

Dear mother/father god, spirit, and universe,

I call on the powers of my highest self, light, love, truth, nature, and healing.

I call on my angels, guides, ancestors, and all those supporting me.

In this moment, I choose gratitude for _____.

I am cultivating a full, golden cup. The golden cup of my being is ever flowing and overflowing with gratitude and joy.

I call on the energies of gratitude, peace, joy, abundance, satisfaction, and contentment. I breathe them into myself and feel them within my whole being and field.

When I look out, I see these energies reflected in my environment.

Any codes, blockages, programs, or agreements preventing me from feeling joy are cleared immediately and in all lifetimes.

I am learning to see from the perspective of a glass overflowing with abundance.

I am learning to trust in all that I have co-created and the places where I have created positive change.

I am learning to focus my attention on what I have, on what is going and working well, and on what's possible.

I am learning to stay in gratitude for all of my blessings.

I have all that I need to feel safe and loved, and to work in my soul purpose.

I am free of the need to manifest, produce, or create anything, or to make anything happen.

I can be at peace with what is.

I am discerning what influences I expose myself to that may trigger illusions of comparison, competition, scarcity, lack,

not-enoughness, and failure. I am transmuting my
relationship to these lower influences.

I am open to seeing what joy means for me in my life.

I choose to believe it's possible for me to experience joy.
To know it in my body, in my relationships, in my home,
and in the world.

I allow myself the experience of joy in all its expressions.

I am learning to witness my own joy.

I am learning to trust how to feel joy.

I'm open to being shown how to balance the sadness, grief,
_____ I feel, with gratitude and joy.

I'm also learning to trust that it's normal to feel down
sometimes.

I am learning that it's okay when I don't feel okay. I welcome
all the states of my emotional rainbow.

I remember that I belong here and everything I feel is okay.

I am learning to trust the ebbs and flows, the expansion and
contraction, the ups and downs.

All channels to feeling and holding gratitude and joy are open
and surrounded in light.

I continually release striving and seeking.

New constructs are being created for me to feel a full range of
joyful emotions.

I build my capacity for gratitude and joy and this strengthens
the field of my loved ones and community.

With deepest gratitude, so be it.

RESTORING THE HEART/SOURCE CONNECTION

Ancestrally, the energetic heart held great significance. In Egyptian alchemy, the funerary rites discarded the brain but preserved the heart soul, or *ab*, as the heart was the key to the afterworld. Upon dying, you would be safely ferried by Anubis to Maat, who would weigh your heart on a scale against a feather. If your heart was lighter than the feather, you would gain entry to life everlasting.

In Tibetan and Traditional Chinese Medicine, the mind is the heart. And the heart holds the spirit, or *shen*.

The Hopi defined harmony as one's heartbeat in resonance with others and the Earth.

Celtic triquetra carvings resembling the heart were thought to represent eternity.

In Sanskrit, the heart is known as the *anahata*, the fourth chakra, and is associated with balance and serenity. It is represented by a lotus flower with twelve petals.

The English word for heart originated from the Latin *cor*, which is also the root of the word *courage*.

Feeling and being love happens throughout the entire body, but most dramatically in and through the heart center. The heart is our strongest tool of resonance, our inner instrument of deep intuition, which helps us to see, hear, feel, know, and sense what is true and real. Heart coherence is "a state of alignment between the heart, mind, emotions, and physical symptoms." A heart operating in coherence is sine waves, undulating evenly and consistently. In contrast, a heart operating in incoherence is choppy, less rhythmic jagged lines.

The primary wound that complex trauma survivors must heal is the secure reattachment to themselves. Articulated another way, the heart or source connection must be restored. Our culture doesn't teach us how to be embodied, to love ourselves, or to value and protect a heart connection—it actually prohibits it. And so, we are all making our way back to ourselves through the heart. Prayer can serve as a magnetic and empowering method for repairing the heart/source connection not just within ourselves, but with one another and the Earth.

> **"It is only with the heart that one can see rightly; what is essential is invisible to the eye."**
>
> —ANTOINE DE SAINT-EXUPÉRY

Reconstellating around the heart is not a task that is to be underestimated. Strange as it may sound, I encounter a lot of confusion around the difference between love and harm, and the role that love plays in our healing, the quality of our lives, and the impact we can have in the world. As with contentment and peace, I think living in one's heart is what many of us are seeking, even if we aren't aware of it.

Love is all. It is trust, it is empowerment, it is clarity, it is balance, it is connection, and it is empowered service. It is the ability to exist in heart/source connection. It is so much, if not all, that we aspire to. Love is the strongest vibration and it carries the greatest power. And we don't get to bypass loving ourselves: If you want to heal, you will have to find a way to love yourself. Loving yourself is not to be confused with being narcissistic, self-absorbed, or self-obsessed. Self-love shouldn't be considered flippant or selfish. Loving oneself fiercely and unconditionally is a prerequisite for real and sustainable change.

True self-love is protective and allows for vulnerability and bravery. It is strengthening, and makes forgiveness, resilience, and solidarity possible. These are all vital for living in our ever-changing world. Maintaining a heart connection ensures our humanity.

I think a lot of times it's easier to love outside of yourself—another person, a friend group, a pet. But when we hold a strong field of love for ourselves, we strengthen and harmonize, and we actualize a new process for change. So many of us are yearning for change—both inner and outer. As bell hooks said, "If you feel that you can't do sh*t about your own reality, how can you really think you could change the world? When you're f*ed-up and you lead the revolution, you are probably going to get a pretty f*ed-up revolution." This is a stark reminder of the critical role self-healing plays in creating positive change, not just for our inner microcosm, but for the larger macrocosm as well. Prayer is an instigator of change, and when we empower ourselves through prayer, we strengthen the channel to our own hearts, initializing the connection of the collective heart.

> **"When a complex system is far from equilibrium, small islands of coherence in a sea of chaos have the capacity to shift the entire system to a higher order."**
>
> —ILYA PRIGOGINE, NOBEL LAUREATE

All these heartbreaks we must cope with in our lives can be reframed as activations for heart connection and break*through*. Restoration of the heart/source connection is vital for us all.

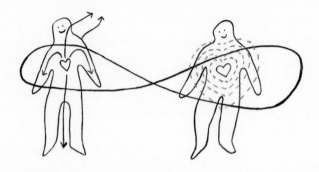

Heart center energy can flow through various channels in the body (left) and also radiate outward (right), emanating from the electromagnetic field around the heart.

HEART IN INCOHERENCE HEART/SOURCE DISCONNECTION	HEART IN COHERENCE HEART/SOURCE CONNECTION
Focused on surface stimuli, reactive to information, cut off from deeper intelligence and wisdom	Accessing both emerging and retrospective wisdom/crystalized intelligence
Overly mental or intellectual, rational but cut off from intelligence of body or intuition	Discernment—ability to synthesize information from mind and body
Disconnected from lower-energy centers; speaking, thinking, and acting detached from heart	Greater inner connectivity—integration between upper and lower body, speaking from heart, thinking from heart, acting from heart; greater synchronization of whole system

Weaker outer connectivity—unsafe to connect, loneliness and isolation, feel separate from life, feel disconnected from or superior to nature	Stronger outer connectivity—heart connections with other people, plants, animals, places, life; feel part of life
Weak resonance, weaker ability to see, hear, feel, and know on deeper level	Strong resonance, for seeing, hearing, feeling, and knowing on deeper level
More difficult to be embodied, more difficult to just be	Embodiment and being states easier to experience, easier to just be
Making decisions from fear, limited judgment, disassociated place	Making decisions from a heart-centered place, fuller judgment, discernment, embodied
Psychophysiologically, more rigidity in heart, narrower window of resilience, greater anxiety or aggression in social relationships	Psychophysiologically, enhanced ability to adapt to challenges, self-regulate, and engage in amicable social relationships
Difficulty giving and receiving compassion, nurturance, peace, and love	Greater ease giving and receiving compassion, nurturance, peace, and love

In attachment-theory terms, the restoration of the heart/source connection is the reestablishment of a secure attachment to our whole selves and the Earth. A secure attachment has many benefits, including: a healthy self-concept, comfort with intimacy, and an easier time emotionally regulating. Healing our attachment to ourselves underlies any interpersonal rupture. When this is achieved, it is then possible that even the deepest, most painful wounds can indeed be healed, regardless of whether a resolution is possible on the physical level.

When our heart/source energy is flowing unhindered, we feel connected with ourselves and in the stream of life. We doubt less and trust more. When we restore the heart/source connection, we reorient around our whole selves. A heart/source connection is necessary for experiencing the highest vibratory states, and also for transmitting them outward. Put another way, this is necessary for giving as well as receiving darshan, a healing emanation.

Heart coherence is a powerful way to resource ourselves for the present and for the future. It's vitally important that we learn how to make decisions from our hearts, as opposed to from fear. It is possible to be so embodied in yourself that there is no space for anything that isn't *for you*. You become crystal clear in your work—what to open to, engage with, take on, and say no to—and this is high discernment. If you are connected to your heart, whatever you choose is the right choice. The universe is not a punishment-reward system; it works according to frequency and vibration, and the cycle of co-creation occurs within the bounds of cosmic law.

Heart Connection Ritual

This is a great exercise to do over time, to observe how your relationship to your heart changes.

Step one) *Create three lines of language to accompany this ritual (e.g., "I'm learning that it's safe to breathe and sense into my heart. I allow myself to trust being in closer relationship with my heart. I invite my heart to relax and receive."). Write down your mantra. Check in with yourself to confirm that the language matches what you're feeling.*

Step two) *Bring your breath into a slow and steady rhythm. Sit quietly with this language and repeat it five to seven times. If sitting quietly isn't an option, you can add some gentle somatic movement such as lying backside down and rocking with your heels; standing and swaying from side to side, letting your arms be heavy and twisting; or sitting with arms crossed, alternately lightly tapping each upper arm.*

Step three) *Notice how you feel in your body. What's different? What feels unchanged? Did you notice any resistance coming up, or places you felt stuck, confused, or critical? Note your findings so you can compare notes next time.*

The Healing Circle

Humans have always circled together, around trees and fires, under the sun and moon, through hardship and abundance. We have always found our way back to each other and the Earth. Things are perpetually falling apart and coming together, and while the center may not be able to hold, the circle can and will.

The mycelial network is an underground system connecting the plants, trees, and fungi. This awe-inspiring matrix of ecosystems functions very much like the extracellular matrix. It not only communicates (via electrical charge), but distributes nutrients, shares resources, stores memory, and can respond and adapt to environmental changes. What is interesting to me about the mycelial network is that it operates and thrives purely integratively—no individual parts are disconnected or left out. It functions holistically, according to what is best for the whole network.

We, too, are intimately connected with this web of life. Now is a time of gathering and building our relationships into strong, vast, and intersecting networks. Now is an important time to expand our circles and trust in the safety, strength, and power of them.

Circling together can be an initiation and an activation. A release and an integration. A surrender and a gathering. In times of stress, we are biologically hardwired to collapse into fight, flight, freeze, or fawn—but we also know how to tend to one another adaptively.

A consistent prayer practice will bring change into your life, and circling together with like-minded friends will amplify that change. However, you must be open to seeing, feeling, and believing change is happening, so you can ultimately *embody and be the change*. Watch what your environment is reflecting back to you. Observe the symbolism, the synchronicity, and what nature reveals to you. Be open to receiving insight in new ways and from new places. Remember the concept of *ayatana*—perception on subtle levels. Where do you see and feel change happening? Can you orient your attention around that? Having others reflect where they observe and feel change is valuable for group work, because individually we have a tendency to get stuck in the same limited loops and sight lines. When the conditions are right, working intentionally with others opens up our minds and hearts, so change can happen organically.

In our capitalist society, all aspects of our survival are geared toward individuality and competition. On the other hand, nature teaches us interdependence. It shows us how to exist together in harmony with our ecosystem. The power of the circle is a counterbalance to the rugged individualism, and personal liberty over collective responsibility, that has greatly fractured us. I am not interested in competition—show me where I can co-create and reveal where connection is possible. The power of the circle ensures that you don't have to figure it out alone. It's not all up to you. There is strength in numbers, especially when you're working co-creatively and the group becomes more than the sum of its parts.

Some tips for facilitating a prayer circle:

- **Set clear intentions. What is the purpose of your circle? What are you here to explore, embody, see together, allow, and create?**

- **Consider atmospherics. Serve tea, light candles or incense, play soft music, and/or create an altar in the center where everyone can place a sacred object to charge during the ceremony.**

- **Consider how and when you will meet. Will it be remotely, in person, or both? Will you choose full or new moons, solstices or equinoxes, or other days that feel sacred to you?**

- **Center safety. Simply stating your circle is a "safe space" is not sufficient. Can you ask people what would encourage them to feel safe? What are some guidelines or rules you want to establish? How is confidentiality ensured? Also, consider the energetics of opening and closing the circle.**

- **Invite wisely.** Is this a closed circle? Or an open one? How will you know who is the right fit for this group? How will you articulate this?

- **Trust in the field.** Prayer circles are wonderful opportunities to see the alchemy of the field working in action. You get to trust that what comes up in these spaces has purpose, and that people can handle it.

- **Make a commitment.** What are you prepared to commit to? Maybe it's simply being present and showing up. Or maybe you're up for challenging your perceptions a little, or processing a particular issue. If your circle is donation-based, consider offering a portion to a worthy cause.

- **Remember that just as prayers are living documents,** prayer circles are works in progress. Everything is an opportunity for growth. How can we honor our intentions in a way that facilitates openness, hope, courage, and awakening?

PRAYER FOR THE NEW EARTH

There are no easy solutions to the complex individual and collective challenges we face on every level in our lifetimes. Prayer work is a mighty ally for us as we navigate the collapses and eventual rebuilding and restoration, which, if we think beyond the limited constructs of time and space, can be simultaneously occurring. At the material level, the destruction is horrifying and heartbreaking. At the level of spirit, it is all an infinite evolution.

Even on my hardest days, when I get caught in despair and hopelessness, I still pray. I don't pray out of desperation, but as an act of surrender. Even when the shadow overtakes me, my prayers mean that I am still bringing my best to the game. I am offering my highest contribution in spirit.

Our being here, right now, is not a coincidence. To my highly empathic ones: Our sensitivities are not an accident or a liability. They have purpose. How can you bring curiosity and creativity to these waves of emotion? They may feel like walls, but look deeper. They are surges carrying great energy of change with them.

I'm no longer asking if I can handle this. Instead I ask:

How am I going to walk this?

What is this an invitation for?

What do I need to find my way through this?

What am I being guided to create within this space?

Where can my resources be of service to me?
My community? The Earth?

Where am I being led to join forces with others?

The prayer space reminds me to stay resolute in the actions I've committed to. Our prayers and commitments aren't something we need to necessarily prepare to do, one day in the future or off in the distance. We can be present with our commitments here and now. This is where we get to put our intentions into action.

What I've learned is that a big part of my work is *remembering* that I am so much more than just a physical body. If we think about the body elementally, we are all four elements, ever changing and interconnected. We are part earth, which is fixed, immutable, and solid. However, we are even more water. The energetics of water are adaptability, receptivity, and flow. As fluid crystalline beings, we are holders, but we are also transmitters. We are air, light and mutable. We are the fire that knows how to ignite, transmute, and shine brightly without burning out. We're not meant to simply hold pain and collapse under the weight of it. We get to move with it. Our planet is in its own cycle of co-creation, as are we. We get to alchemize our intentions and resolutions, to work with them elementally.

If you want to work elementally with what you're feeling, maybe you let yourself weep (water), move (water and fire), make an offering (air), and use that emotion and put it into action (fire). Maybe you alchemize with other people and groups. We're not meant to take all this on and hold it alone. No single one of us can save the Earth, but we can pick a ray of the rainbow that is within our reach.

We are being asked to hold a unified state of balance, despite increasing imbalance. This is an education that, at times, feels like too much, but we have the opportunity to trust that we were made for everything that's unfolding here and now.

As you take what resonates from this book, I hope you, too, will remember your connection to the divine, the Earth, and your own heart. I hope you will hold a new reverence for the power that lies in your prayers. May you remember and reclaim everything you need in order to celebrate your whole rainbow body being. May this remembrance awaken the parts of you and your awareness that connect you to whatever you choose. May you feel empowered to trust yourself in the deepest and subtlest of ways. May this reconstellation allow you to fully embody yourself and inhabit your life, in perfect heart alignment. And may this reorientation bring you exactly where you need to be.

PRAYER FOR THE NEW EARTH

Dear mother/father god, spirit, and universe,

I call on the powers of my highest self, light, love, truth, nature, and healing.

I call on my angels, guides, ancestors, and all those supporting me.

I call for the immediate and infinite protection of all sentient beings.

I pray for the highest healing of Mother Earth, the plants and animals, the elements.

I weep for the Earth but I trust in the infinite wisdom of it, the potential of cosmic consciousness, and resilience far beyond the destruction of man.

I pray for the highest healing of the collective.

I pray for the end of oppression.

I pray for oppressed peoples to reclaim their autonomy.

I pray for the equitable redistribution of resources, for the true stewards, caretakers, way showers, and wisdom keepers to come into power.

Protect all the children here and coming in.

May all beings be safe, healthy, and free.

It's okay if I don't know what to do; the Earth does.

I trust that a rebalancing is underway, beyond our knowing.

I trust that we have not been forsaken, but rather we are supported by life in many dimensions, in the past, present, and future, here and beyond the limited constructs of what we know as here.

The ancestors are with us, none of their struggle has been in vain.

I choose to trust in this tempering.

To be aware, but not afraid.

I release as much of my old fear/unconsciousness programming
as I am able at this time.

I call in all my light, all my power, to trust it and know it.

I connect with all those who are using their power for good.

May we find ways to transmute hopelessness, powerlessness,
and despair into hope, awakening, and possibility.

May we remember we are always connected to source, which is
pure love, and have the opportunity to co-create with this
infinite energy.

May our collective tears be transmuted into something greater
than a river of grief, into something as grand and beautiful
as we can dream together.

I can't take on the shadow of everything, nor can I fix it. But I am
clear on what I need to be accountable for.

I am in my discernment with what I expose myself to, especially
all forms of online media.

I allow myself to get completely clear about my work here and now.

May we learn how to hold all of this.

May we learn to stay open for this while staying connected to
ourselves.

Following as well as leading, speaking as well as listening.

I see what I need to see and move with it.

I am resourced to be fully here, to be of deep service.

Doing none of this perfectly but as I am.

I allow myself to be held and supported.

May we be able to bear what is here and what comes.

The best way I can prepare for the future is to exist fully in
the present.

When the pain feels like too much, may I remember that my
heart is being activated along with many people who share
this grief.

I allow myself to feel whatever I need to.

May we find ways to move through the pain, remain open, and
allow it to flow through as it needs to, and be released back
to the Earth and to the light.

May this pain support our actions for and commitments to
the Earth.

What is ahead is not what came before.

I have no need to brace myself for life.

I have no need to hide, because I know the truth.

May we enter a different time, full of peace and love.

I passed the test.

I broke the spell.

This is the new present moment, where all things are possible.

It's safe for me to be fully here; there is maximum protection in
being fully present.

I open all of my sensory perceptions with high discernment to
guide and protect me.

I give myself complete permission to be fully in my trusting,
knowing, visioning, and being.

May we open to this powerful time of remembering: our true
selves and the cosmic laws.

May we reconnect and open to all channels of vibratory states,
especially joy, power, and resilience.

Any part of myself that underestimated me is lovingly
integrated into my being.

Any voice that undermines or underestimates me is cleared
from my field.

There is no good or bad. Everything has a purpose.

Please help me to be of the highest service in bringing the Earth
and all sentient beings into the highest harmony. I pray we
all get to evolve into the New Earth, where all beings are safe,
healthy, and free.

With deepest gratitude, so be it.

ACKNOWLEDGMENTS

This book came to and through me co-creatively with the help of many people, beings, blessings, and energies. Gratitude to my spirit team: my angels, guides, and ancestors. Gratitude to nature and the elements. Gratitude to the plants and animals, for your pure beingness.

Thank you to ~

My biological family, my original teachers. My brother, Stuart, for lighting my way. My beloved universe partner, Will, for having my back in every way, and for seeing me as a writer way before I could. My grandmother Jane, for always encouraging me to write and create. Sherie, for always encouraging me to be me. My spirit mother and teacher, Jane, for the eternal love and guidance. My literary agent, Meg, for being the best and always knowing what to do. Chelsea, for your brilliance and openness; creating with you is a dream. Shannon, for challenging me and holding the most amazing space for this project. Running Press, for taking a chance on me and seeing the possibility in this book. To Hallie C., for sharing your experience and brilliant ideas so generously, and for genuinely working toward making the world a better place.

My clients, for constantly challenging and inspiring me. My European Dissent group, PISAB, and SURJ, for opening my eyes and keeping me accountable. Sheri Heller, for your peerless guidance, scholarship, and commitment to helping trauma survivors. To all my colleagues, for your comfort, insights, collaboration, and connection. Raven, Hilda, Linda, David G., and Lawson, for your guidance from the invisible realms. My plant medicine teachers: Patricia and Richard Katz, David Dalton, Lindsay Fauntelroy, Judith Peolarends, Claudia Keel, Richard Mandelbaum, Karen Rose, Lata Chettri-Kennedy. My plant medicine and flower friends, the American Herbalist Guild, the Flower Essence Society, and the Mutual Aid Herbalists of New York.

To all of my soul family and friends, who not only support me unconditionally in my creative pursuits, but ensure my survival here as well. Cate, for always keeping it real and also hilarious. Liza, for Post-it notes on the beach and for your deep maternal wisdom. To Deborah, for always keeping it human, embodied, and Earthly. My moon sister, Natalia, for your bright spirit and love. Keely, for your loving voice and all the ways you share and create. Rebeca, for your clarity, warmth, and kindness. Crista, for being in my corner, personally and professionally. Jennye, for your perspective and general consciousness level, which I value greatly. Nicole, for your honesty and courage in facing this crazy world. Karyn, for helping me see healthier ways of relating to myself and the world. Sarah M., for the nourishment: sweet as well as spiritual. Kalen, for your artistry and vision. Jason and Amanda, for being badasses and teaching me about the creative process. Mark Anthony, for all the care, love, and laughter. Sara N., for the light bulbs of expertise you share generously. Kim F., for ideating and creating in all realms. Nick and Jenni, for helping me grow through love and laughter. Rebecca K., for your exquisite voice in all its dimensions. Alexa, for being a warrior goddess. Penelope, for your commitment to healing and sharing your wisdom here. Vanessa, for helping me find my voice and channel it more strongly. Malissa, for being a fierce witch and kind soul. Bill, for being a solid bro. Gretchen, for your spiritual business acumen and reminding me to RYB. Marie, for always being here for workshopping and processing. Concetta, for being up for one hell of a ride. Anna-Maria, for making this world a safer and more loving place. Emily, for your perspective and help in shifting mine. Herpreet, for your intellect and bravery. Ana, for always wanting to play and learn in nature with me. Virginia, for being in the heart space of possibility with me.

To all of the wise women and humans who protected the mystery teachings through the ages. To all those with a commitment to protecting the plants, animals, and the Earth. To the changemakers doing the brave work of dismantling and rebuilding toward greater equity and peace from a heart-centered place.

GLOSSARY

Alchemy: an inner process of transformation

Alignment: the process of coming into cosmic balance, a state of harmony within the self and in one's environment, also known as ascending

Attachment style: type of care we receive from our caregivers as infants and children; corresponds to how we feel in relationship with ourselves, with others, and our world. There are four types of attachment: secure, anxious, avoidant, and disorganized. A secure attachment is also a heart/source connection.

Attunement: process of making deep contact with another realm or spirit, usually a plant or stone, e.g., attuning with a plant allows one to connect with the consciousness of that plant spirit, gaining insight into how it works, how it wants to help, etc.

Bypass: process of sub- or unconsciously avoiding dealing with an issue, usually because tolerating the distress is too painful

Capitalism: patriarchal economic system wherein a group's trade and industry are privately owned, instead of publicly owned; a system of scarcity that rewards the dominant culture

Chakra system: a system of energy centers along the central axis of the body that are connected to both the physical and subtle bodies via energetic pathways; also connected with the meridians and nadis. There are seven chakras: root, sacral, solar plexus, heart, throat, third eye, and crown. This system closely resembles the hormonal centers of the endocrine system.

Christian hegemony: the pervasive and systemic set of Christian values, beliefs, and institutions that dominate our society as well as our perception of the sacred through the social, political, economic, and political power they wield

Co-creation: the relational and collaborative process of consciously creating with life

Collective consciousness: the shared beliefs and psycho-spiritual functioning level of the general population

Consciousness: a state of awareness that can occur in multiple levels and dimensions simultaneously and is not limited by time or space. Everything with a vibrational signature possesses consciousness—this includes but is not limited to: the elements, the ocean, the cosmos, places, memories, disease, feeling states, plants, stones, and animals.

Cosmic: relating to the universe and the governing principles held therein

Cultural appropriation: the stealing or borrowing from a culture, usually by a member of a dominant culture from a minority culture, without asking for permission, giving credit, or offering compensation; taken inappropriately for one's own personal gain, and can include artwork, intellectual property, and practices

Decolonization: the act of restoring a group's or practice's independence and sovereignty; freeing one's understanding of sociocultural effects of colonization

Discernment: the practice of synchronizing the heart, mind, and higher knowing to make decisions and energetic investments

Dismantling: the act of taking apart harmful structures, such as belief systems

Duality: binary of opposites; dual thinking holds that something must be "either/or" instead of "both/and"; e.g., something can be shadow or light

Elements: arising out of the ancient Greek and Asian concepts for air, earth, fire, and water; each has a corresponding spirit, called an elemental

Empath: a highly sensitive individual who may have enhanced clairvoy-ant, clairaudient, and/or clairsentient abilities; individuals especially vulnerable to taking on the negative affect, conflict, and/or suffering of other beings and the collective

Energetic: refers to the subtle, vibrational, emotional, or bioelectric charge of something, e.g., a plant or state of consciousness

Extracellular matrix: biocrystalline structures that form networks within the body and are made up of interstitial fluid, fascia, cell salts, fatty tissues, lymph tissue, red and white blood cells, and the pineal gland.

These physical structures interact with the subtle bodies to transmit information.

Flower essence: a vibrational plant medicine made from flowers placed in water and a small amount of preservative, which can be used to address a wide variety of emotional, mental, and spiritual, as well as physical, conditions and situations

Frequency: a vibrational measurement; describes the number of waves that pass a fixed point in a set amount of time divided into octaves. All matter has frequency.

Grounding: a protective and restorative practice that is the process of attuning one's energy with the Earth's frequency; can be enhanced by utilizing breathwork, visualization, and flower essences

Holographic principle: a theoretical framework, which holds that every piece contains the whole and can create an energy interference pattern; every cell within the human body contains the information to create an entire duplicate body; "As above, so below"

Institutional racism: racism expressed systemically at the socio-political level that informs the disparity around healthcare, income, and criminal justice among other factors; can be difficult to observe due to its ingrained and subtle characteristics within the dominant culture

Intention: the declaration, goal, or vision for a desired outcome

Intersectionality: the interconnectedness of gender, sexual orientation, race, class, ethnicity, ability, and culture

Macrocosm: the whole system; also universe or cosmos; the macrocosm has a reciprocal relationship with the microcosm

Manifestation: the process of encouraging a desired outcome through intention

Matriarchy: a system ruled by and organized around women

Metaphysical: quantum model of understanding concerned with energy, light, and vibration; characteristic of an indigenized worldview

Microcosm: part of the whole; humans are a part of the universe; the microcosm has a reciprocal relationship with the macrocosm

Mystery schools: an ancient collective, or school, with its own sacred teachings; the wisdom of these schools is handed down through various lineages for the purpose of evolution

Newtonian physics: an orientation of understanding reality through mechanical events and matter; concerned with understanding the universe primarily according to physical structure

Nonduality or nondualism: terms that originate from Buddhist, Hindu, and Taoist teachings, many indigenous and shamanic teachings, and various esoteric and mystical texts; means oneness

Patriarchy: a system ruled by and organized around men, which reinforces heteronormativity; the current pervading system of power in our world

Physical body: the gross, corporeal self; depends on the etheric body for survival

Plant signature: the way in which a plant has adapted to its environment and assumes certain forms; the plant's personality

Polarity: one of two sides of something; can be positive or negative

Prayer: an active agreement that you make between your soul and the divine (whatever that means to you); a sacred practice that can be called upon to bring about states of grace, healing, and change. Prayer can also be: meditation, spell, wish, incantation, and affirmation.

Program: a set of internalized beliefs we interpret as true; determines much of how we function

Quantum mechanics: also sometimes referred to as quantum physics, a scientific framework that aims to define physical phenomena beyond the subatomic level

Ritual: an intentional practice with a therapeutic purpose

Sacred geometry: refers to the patterns found within structures of the natural world as well as in human-made structures of sacred art and architecture; correlates to the harmonics, or resonant frequencies, found in music, light, and cosmology

Shadow work: engaging part of the unconscious, or shadow, for greater integration and healing

Source: our connection to the undifferentiated self, heart, spirit, universe, the divine, or however you define the sacred

Source connection: a secure attachment, or heart connection; the internal blueprint that maps how source energy runs through you. Source connection is constant, unbreakable, and always available to us.

Subconscious: between the conscious and the unconscious; what has been suppressed

Subtle: referring to energy, matter, and the bodies at a higher frequency or resonance than the physical, more dense level

Subtle body/bodies: those psycho-spiritual planes of the self that exist outside the physical body, including the etheric, astral, mental, and causal; they are distinct layers but are connected via energetic pathways

Thought forms: conscious or unconscious thoughts existing in the astral and mental body; may have emotional intensity, making them denser

Unconscious: what we don't know; deep in the void

Vibrational: the energetic quality of something; associated with and can be measured at the level of frequency; term is sometimes used interchangeably with energetic and subtle energetic

Vibrational medicine: sometimes called subtle energetic medicine; uses specialized forms of energy to positively affect those energetic systems that may be out of balance due to disease states

Vitalism: energy that inhabits and influences the physical body; similar to the concept of qi in Traditional Chinese Medicine, prana in Ayurveda, and vital force in homeopathy, ashé in Yoruba

White supremacy: the belief that white people are racially superior and should dominate society and the Earth, typically to the exclusion and/or detriment of other racial and ethnic groups

NOTES

I.

Bessel van der Kolk, *The Body Keeps the Score: Brain, Mind, and Body in the Healing of Trauma* (New York: Penguin Books, 2014).

studies involving mantra, affirmation, meditation: Andrew Newberg and Mark Robert Waldman, *How God Changes Your Brain: Breakthrough Findings from a Leading Neuroscientist* (New York: Ballantine Books, 2010).

II.

"Prayer is listening to the silence of one's own heart": Sherry Ruth Anderson, *The Feminine Face of God* (New York: Bantam, 1992).

"Sri Ma Anandamayi Sri Ma's Teachings." n.d. Accessed September 14, 2023. https://www.anandamayi.org/sri-sri-mas-teachings/#:~:text=A%20 fixed%20time%20for%20prayer.

"Attention, taken to its highest degree": Simone Weil, Emma Crawford, Mario Von, and Gustave Thibon, *Gravity and Grace* (New York: Routledge, 2008).

Seren Bertrand and Azra Bertrand, *Magdalene Mysteries* (Rochester: Bear & Co., 2020).

"Prayer can be like drawing water": "Perseverance Made Teresa of Avila a Master of Prayer," 2015. Denver Catholic, March 28, 2015, https:// denvercatholic.org/perseverance-made-teresa-avila-master-prayer/.

According to a Pew Research Center survey: "Religious Landscape Study," Pew Research Center's Religion & Public Life Project, https:// www.pewresearch.org/religion/religious-landscape-study/ frequency-of-prayer/.

Maasai women prostrate themselves: "Maasai Blessing Ceremony for Fertility and Rain, Images and Description," n.d. Influentialpoints.com, https://influentialpoints.com/Gallery/Maasai_Blessing_Ceremony.htm.

"One should only pray that another": Etty Hillesum, *Letters from Westerbork* (London: Grafton, 1988).

Many know that Thoth was the god of writing: Joyce A. Tyldesley, *Daughters of Isis: Women of Ancient Egypt* (New York: Penguin, 1995).

In East Asia, ancestor worship: Valeska Gehrmann, "Ancestor Worship in Taoism—Chinese Customs," 2019, Nationsonline.org, https://www.nationsonline.org/oneworld/Chinese_Customs/taoism_ancestor_worship.htm.

Ikebana, the prayerful act of arranging flowers: Maggie Oman Shannon, *The Way We Pray* (Newburyport: Conari Press, 2001).

In Australia, Aboriginal prayers: Artlandish Aboriginal Art Gallery, "What Is Aboriginal Dreamtime?" April 2, 2019, https://www.aboriginal-art-australia.com/aboriginal-art-library/aboriginal-dreamtime/.

If healing is needed: Joseph Bruchac, *Four Ancestors: Stories, Songs, and Poems from Native North America* (Mahwah: Bridgewater Books, 1996).

"A balance should be struck": Paramahansa Yogananda, *Scientific Healing Affirmations* (Los Angeles: Self Realization Fellowship, 1958).

"When we pray, I think that we can be led": "Maya Angelou's Prayer and Meditation Practice!" November 5, 2018, https://www.curlynikki.com/2018/11/maya-angelous-prayer-and-meditation.html.

Neuroimaging (SPECT, PET, and MRI): Andrew B. Newberg. 2014. "The Neuroscientific Study of Spiritual Practices," *Frontiers in Psychology* 5 (March), https://doi.org/10.3389/fpsyg.2014.00215.

Scientists have determined that praying involves: Nicole Spector, "This Is Your Brain on Prayer and Meditation," October 20, 2017, NBC News, https://www.nbcnews.com/better/health/your-brain-prayer-meditation-ncna812376.

Comparably, spirituality and meditative practices: Patty Van Cappellen, Baldwin M. Way, Suzannah F. Isgett, and Barbara L. Fredrickson. 2016. "Effects of Oxytocin Administration on Spirituality and Emotional Responses to Meditation," *Social Cognitive and Affective Neuroscience* 11 (10): 1579–1587, https://doi.org/10.1093/scan/nsw078.

It has also been linked to reducing fear: P. Kirsch. 2005. "Oxytocin Modulates Neural Circuitry for Social Cognition and Fear in Humans," *Journal of Neuroscience* 25 (49): 11489–11493, https://doi.org/10.1523/jneurosci.3984-05.2005.

Evidence suggests that prayer is protective: Andrew B. Newberg. 2011. "Spirituality and the Aging Brain," *Generations: Journal of the American Society on Aging* 35 (2): 83–91, https://www.jstor.org/stable/26555779.

And given the way prayer and meditation: Jeffrey Rediger, *Cured: The Life-Changing Science of Spontaneous Healing* (New York: Flatiron Books, 2021).

Meditating on or studying any subject is good: Andrew Newberg and Mark Robert Waldman, *How God Changes Your Brain: Breakthrough Findings from a Leading Neuroscientist* (New York: Ballantine Books, 2010).

"decreased anxiety and fearfulness": Roland R. Griffiths, Matthew W. Johnson, William A. Richards, Brian D. Richards, Robert Jesse, Katherine A. MacLean, Frederick S. Barrett, Mary P. Cosimano, and Maggie A. Klinedinst. 2017. "Psilocybin-Occasioned Mystical-Type Experience in Combination with Meditation and Other Spiritual Practices Produces Enduring Positive Changes in Psychological Functioning and in Trait Measures of Prosocial Attitudes and Behaviors," *Journal of Psychopharmacology* 32 (1): 49–69, https://doi.org/10.1177/0269881117731279.

When the prefrontal cortex enters this state: Mihaly Csikszentmihalyi, *Flow: The Psychology of Optimal Experience* (New York: Harper and Row, 1990).

Deafferentation initiates a neural cascade: E. Mohandas. 2008. "Neurobiology of Spirituality," *Mens Sana Monographs* 6 (1): 63, https://doi.org/10.4103/0973-1229.33001.

Deepak Chopra describes the process: Deepak Chopra, *Quantum Healing: Exploring the Frontiers of Mind/Body Medicine* (New York: Random House, 2007).

"Indians believe that one cannot fool": Jack D. Forbes, *Columbus and Other Cannibals: The Wetiko Disease of Exploitation, Imperialism, and Terrorism* (New York: Seven Stories Press, 2008).

"There is an electrical current": Thich Nhat Hanh and Rachel Neumann, *The Energy of Prayer: How to Deepen Your Spiritual Practice* (Berkeley: Parallax Press, 2006).

coined in the 1960s by Dr. Hans Jenny: Hans Jenny, *Cymatics: A Study of Wave Phenomena and Vibration* (Edinburgh: Macromedia, 2007).

Frequency **describes the number of waves:** Heidi Smith, *The Bloom Book: A Flower Essence Guide to Cosmic Balance* (Louisville: Sounds True, 2020).

Resonance **is the process:** James L. Oschman, *Energy Medicine: The Scientific Basis* (Edinburgh: Elsevier, 2016).

Harmonics **are "multiples of the fundamental frequency":** Ibid.

He also studied water that emerged: Masaru Emoto, *The Hidden Messages in Water* (New York: Atria Books, 2005).

When your neurophysiology hears: Tom Kenyon, "Sound Healing Intensive." Lecture, September 30, 2017, Seattle, WA.

"Prayer, sitting with a picture of a holy being": Ram Dass, "Devotion to the Beloved," January 28, 2015, https://www.ramdass.org/devotion-to-beloved/.

It contains no active plant constituents: Richard Gerber and William A. Teller, *Vibrational Medicine: The #1 Handbook of Subtle-Energy Therapies* (Rochester: Bear & Co., 2001).

"Each cell in the body": Matthew Wood, *Holistic Medicine and the Extracellular Matrix* (New York: Simon and Schuster, 2021).

fascia and ECM *determine* **the environment:** Oschman, *Energy Medicine*.

"due to the way it is structured": Penelope McDonnell, "Prayer and the Extracellular Matrix Interview," by Heidi Smith, Summer 2023.

In TCM, air is associated with metal: Alaine D. Duncan and Kathy L. Kain, *The Tao of Trauma: A Practitioner's Guide for Integrating Five Element Theory and Trauma Treatment* (Berkeley: North Atlantic Books, 2019).

Smith describes the creative potential: Chloe Cooper Jones, "The Radical Hope of Patti Smith," *Harper's Bazaar*, November 28, 2022.

spaces and transmutations inside the brain: G. Marx and C. Gilon. 2012. "The Molecular Basis of Memory," *ACS Chemical Neuroscience* 3 (8): 633–642, https://doi.org/10.1021/cn300097b.

What we perceive as solid matter: Richard Gerber and William A. Teller, *Vibrational Medicine: The #1 Handbook of Subtle Energy Therapies* (Rochester: Bear & Co, 2001).

"frozen light": Michael Talbot, *The Holographic Universe* (New York: Harper Perennial, 1991).

phenomenon now known as the *observer effect*: Rediger, *Cured.*

distant healing and intercessory prayer are effective: Larry Dossey, *Healing Words: The Power of Prayer and the Practice of Medicine* (New York: HarperOne, 1993).

Maharishi International University conducted: Guy D. Hatchard, Ashley J. Deans, Kenneth L. Cavanaugh, and David W. Orme-Johnson. 1996. "The Maharishi Effect: A Model for Social Improvement. Time Series Analysis of a Phase Transition to Reduced Crime in Merseyside Metropolitan Area," *Psychology, Crime & Law* 2 (3): 165–174, https://doi: 10.1080/10683169608409775.

indigenous worldview is validated: Renee Linklater, *Decolonizing Trauma Work: Indigenous Stories and Strategies* (Nova Scotia: Fernwood Publishing, 2014).

"The human being is a house of prayer": Hildegard von Bingen and Beverly Mayne Kienzle, *Homilies on the Gospels* (Collegeville: Cistercian Publications, 2011).

their book *Scriptures, Shrines, Scapegoats, and World Politics*: Zeev Maoz and Errol A. Henderson, "Religion and Quality of Life," In *Scriptures, Shrines, Scapegoats, and World Politics: Religious Sources of Conflict and Cooperation in the Modern Era*, 344–369 (Ann Arbor: University of Michigan Press, 2020).

approximately 70 percent of the world's population: Showing Up for Racial Justice community meeting, October 2022.

era was an inflection point in Europe: Silvia Federici, *Caliban and the Witch* (New York: Autonomedia, 2004).

III.

Highly sensitive persons: Sofie Boterberg and Petra Warreyn. 2016. "Making Sense of It All: The Impact of Sensory Processing Sensitivity on Daily Functioning of Children," *Personality and Individual Differences* 92: 80–86, https://doi.org/10.1016/j.paid.2015.12.022.

"was spiritual protection": Karen Rose, *The Art & Practice of Spiritual Herbalism: Transform, Heal, & Remember with the Power of Plants and Ancestral Medicine* (Beverly, Fair Winds, 2022).

Focusing is a "body-oriented process": Ann Weiser Cornell, *The Power of Focusing: A Practical Guide to Emotional Self-Healing* (Oakland: New Harbinger, 1996).

In polyvagal theory: Stephen W. Porges, *The Polyvagal Theory: Neurophysiological Foundations of Emotions, Attachment, Communication, and Self-Regulation* (New York: W.W. Norton & Co., 2011).

In the Druidic tradition: Hugh Milne, *The Heart of Listening: A Visionary Approach to Craniosacral Work, Vol. 1: Origins, Destination Points, Unfoldment* (Berkeley: North Atlantic Books, 1998).

Wonder and awe are healing: Gina Simmons Schneider, "Healing Trauma with Awe and Wonder," *Psychology Today*, November 5, 2021.

Edward Bruce Bynum, *Our African Unconscious: The Black Origins of Mysticism and Psychology* (Rochester: Inner Traditions, 2021).

Isla Macleod, *Rituals for Life: A Guide to Creating Meaningful Rituals Inspired by Nature* (London: Lawrence King Publishing, 2022).

wisdom is all inside, a crystalized: Arthur C. Brooks, *From Strength to Strength: Finding Success, Happiness, and Deep Purpose in the Second Half of Life* (New York: Portfolio, 2022).

One of our group assignments: https://www.c-span.org/video/?c4804332/
user-clip-conspirators.

"First, they came to take our land and water": Myke Johnson. 2017. "Wanting to Be Indian: When Spiritual Searching Turns into Cultural Theft,"
Wabanaki Reach, https://www.wabanakireach.org/wanting_to_be_
indian_when_spiritual_searching_turns_into_cultural_theft.

Reverend Myke Johnson wants us not to see: Ibid.

"most powerful times to approach a well": Mary Evert Hopman, *Scottish
Herbs and Fairy Lore* (Green Valley Lake: Pendraig Publishing, 2010).

IV.

Alan Watts, *Tao: The Watercourse Way* (New York: Pantheon, 1975).

relationship between yin and yang: Alain D. Duncan and Kathy L. Kain,
*The Tao of Trauma: A Practitioner's Guide for Integrating Five Element Theory
and Trauma Treatment* (Berkeley: North Atlantic Books, 2019).

represents a symbolic devouring of life: Jack D. Forbes, *Columbus and Other
Cannibals: The Wetiko Disease of Exploitation, Imperialism, and Terrorism*
(New York: Seven Stories Press, 2008).

known as memory reconsolidation: Bruce Ecker and Alexandre Vaz. 2022.
"Memory Reconsolidation and the Crisis of Mechanism in Psychotherapy," *New Ideas in Psychology* 66.

According to flower essence pioneer Gurudas: Gurudas, *Flower Essences
and Vibrational Healing* (Los Angeles: Cassandra Press, 1983).

Our ancestral liquid matrix is seawater: Mauro Zapaterra. 2023. "Cerebral Spinal Fluid and Our Connection to Source," Lecture, Science and
Nonduality, YouTube, May 24, 2023.

During sleep: Oliver Cameron Reddy and Ysbrand D. van der Werf.
2020. "The Sleeping Brain: Harnessing the Power of the Glymphatic
System Through Lifestyle Choices," *Brain Sciences* 10 (11): 868, https://
doi:10.3390/brainsci10110868.

there have never been more awakened souls: Clarissa Pinkola Estés, "Do Not Lose Heart, We Were Made for These Times," *Moon Magazine*, 2016, http://moonmagazine.org/clarissa-pinkola-estes-do-not-lose-heart -we-were-made-for-these-times-2016-12-31.

consistent gratitude practice can actually help: "Giving Thanks Can Make You Happier," Harvard Health Publishing, August 14, 2021, https:// www.health.harvard.edu/healthbeat/giving-thanks-can-make -you-happier.

Gratitude can reduce rumination: Philip Watkins, Dean L. Grimm, and Russell L. Kolts. 2004. "Counting Your Blessings: Positive Memories Among Grateful Persons," *Current Psychology* 23 (1): 52–67.

Heart coherence is "a state of alignment": Rollin McCraty and Doc Childre. 2010. "Coherence: Bridging Personal, Social, and Global Health," *Alternative Therapies in Health and Medicine* 16 (4): 12–24.

"you are probably going to get a pretty f*ed-up revolution": Barry Boyce, "Love Fights the Power," Lion's Roar, February 23, 2017, https://www.lionsroar.com/love-fights-the-power.

"a complex system is far from equilibrium": HeartMath Inc.,"Understanding Coherence Tech to Activate Your Larger Intelligence," 2022.

IMAGE CREDITS

Artist unknown. *Abenaki Couple.* Eighteenth Century. Watercolor. City of Montreal Records Management & Archives, Montreal, Canada. https://en.m.wikipedia.org/wiki/File:Abenakis.jpg, p. 34.

Tansley, David V. *Subtle Body: Essence and Shadow (Art and Imagination).* 1977. Print. Thames & Hudson, London, p. 60.

Griemiller, Jaroš. *Nozze alchemiche tra Sole e Luna.* 1578. Print. https://commons.wikimedia.org/wiki/File:Marriage_Sun_Moon_-_Rosarium_Philosophorum_Griemiller.jpg, p. 69.

Torrents, Jordi. *11 Hz vibrating in water.* 2015. Photograph. https://commons.wikimedia.org/wiki/File:Water_under_11_Hz_vibration.jpg, p. 106.

Artist unknown. *Bodhisattva Avalokitesvara.* Ninth century. Sculpture. Height 42 in., width 14 in. National Museum, New Delhi, India. https://commons.wikimedia.org/wiki/File:Khasarpana_Lokesvara.jpg, p. 118.

Linnaeus' floral clock, via Getty Images, p. 147.

Nascimento, Davi. *Nanã Buruku an Orisha of Candomblé.* Year unknown. https://commons.wikimedia.org/wiki/File:Nana_Buruku.jpg, p. 149.

INDEX